HOW TO UNDERSTAND
FINANCIAL
STATEMENTS

UNEWC

James O Gill

KOGAN
PAGE

First published in the United States of America in 1990 entitled *Understanding Financial Statements* by Crisp Publications Inc, 95 First Street, Los Altos, California 94022, USA.

This edition first published in Great Britain in 1991 by Kogan Page Ltd, 120 Pentonville Road, London N1 9JN

British Library Cataloguing in Publication Data

A CIP record for this book is available from the British Library.

ISBN 0-7494-0423-X

Typeset by the Castlefield Press, Wellingborough, Northants.
Printed and bound in Great Britain by Biddles Limited, Guildford.

Contents

Introduction

This book was written for those not familiar with basic financial analysis. Its purpose is to explain fundamental concepts in a clear and understandable way and to provide simple tools that can help readers apply what has been learned to their business needs or interests.

How to Understand Financial Statements is not highly technical. It is also *not* a complete text on financial analysis. There are several excellent books that provide more sophisticated analytical techniques. Because of its simplicity, several liberties have been taken with 'pure' financial definitions to achieve clarity. However all definitions are basically correct. If you choose to delve further into financial analysis you will learn that there are several variations of accounting methods that will provide fine tuning to the basic concepts you obtain from this book.

The material presented in the following pages while not complex, will take some time to master. It is suggested that you first skim through the book to obtain an overview of the material and then start again from the beginning. Going step by step and using the blank forms to work out your own ratios and percentages will give you confidence. By the time you have completed this book, you should have achieved control techniques that will work in your business.

James O Gill

About This Book

This book is written not only for new business owners or operators, but also for those who want better control over the business they manage.

During financial seminars, small business managers frequently mention their difficulties in coming to grips with the financial side of their businesses. These individuals have often been successful in establishing a business, but have been searching for the financial tools that will enable them to be in control. A business is often described in anatomical terms: management is the brain, marketing is the muscle, and finance is the blood. Without the financial aspects (such as a flow of cash) the brain becomes uncommunicative and the muscle unresponsive. Understanding the basics of finance (including the proper control of cash), is essential if any business is to survive and succeed.

Starting a business requires an idea, some self-confidence, and some initial funding. Not much more. Staying in business (ie becoming successful) requires financial management. For example, it is essential to know how to interpret a balance sheet and a profit and loss account. These financial tools tell you how to control your business and make it perform the way you expect.

Over half of all new businesses (excluding franchises), fail within four years. Another 30 percent don't last 10 years. Many of the survivors stay in business, but stagnate without reaching their full potential. Often, a lack of capital is cited as the reason why a business failed. This reason is often true of potentially successful businesses that have no trouble obtaining customers. Ironically, quick but uncontrolled success has caused the downfall of thousands of businesses because the owners or managers were unaware of the financial reasons for their success and blindly over-expanded.

The financial information and techniques presented in this book can help a small business person understand *what* is happening, *why* it is happening, *what* to do, and *when* to do it to make things happen the way you want them to happen.

You will cover basic strategies and simple analytical tools that can help you to:

- Discover what your business is doing compared to similar businesses
- Determine financially whether you are making progress each quarter or year and understand why
- Develop a financial plan for the future.

This book is a reference manual. There is no need to memorise the contents. More emphasis should be placed on thinking about your business as you develop and compare ratios. The page-by-page layout of ratios (and other tools) will enable you to refer to those that are significant to your business at the time you want to use them. Not all the ratios and techniques are meant to be used every time you check the health of your business or decide a future strategy, but you should be aware of those most applicable to your situation.

You will be introduced to 11 standard ratios. As a general rule, several will be significant once a month, others will be important once a year. Still others will be useful as your business grows. These ratios are for you to apply when they are right for you. There is no hard and fast rule concerning when to use ratios, they are simply tools that can help you succeed.

This book will help you learn to:

- Understand and evaluate the role of finance in your business
- Recognise the difference between cash and profit
- Know when borrowing makes sense and will provide tips about dealing with your bank
- Understand what a balance sheet and profit and loss account *really* show

9

- Know where to obtain data that are significant for your business
- Compare your organisation with your competitors or industry
- Predict the future from past trends
- Get more productivity from your organisation's expenses
- Understand basic financial terms when you read about them or hear others use them.

It is important for any business owner, whether new or old, to understand where the business is making money and where it is not. This is the function of finance. Knowing the basics of business finance will enable you to make more money during good times and lose less during bad periods, through practising appropriate planning and decision making.

Other ways of using this book

How to Understand Financial Statements (and the other self-improvement books in this series) can be used effectively in a number of ways. Here are some possibilities:

- *Self-study.* Because the book is self-instructional, all that is needed is a quiet place, some time and a pencil. By completing the activities and exercises, you will not only get valuable feedback, but also practical ideas for self-improvement.
- *Workshops and seminars.* The book is ideal for preparatory reading for a workshop or seminar. With the basics already understood, the quality of participation will improve. More time can then be spent on extending and applying the concepts during the sessions. The book can also be effective when distributed at the beginning of a session, providing both structure and content for the training.
- *Open learning.* Copies can be sent to those not able to attend centralised training sessions.

There are other possibilities, depending on the objectives, programme and ideas of the user. One thing is certain: even after it has been read, this book will serve as excellent reference material which can be easily revised.

Goals

The goals of this book are to:

1. Describe how balance sheets and profit and loss accounts are prepared and what each means to a business.
2. Introduce simple ratios and proportions and show how easily they can be developed and used to derive more meaning from a balance sheet and profit and loss account.
3. Explain how to examine expenses and provide proven ways to help you get better productivity from your expenses.
4. Provide four tested techniques that will enable you to exercise better control over your business finances.

This book is designed to help you meet the above goals by taking you through the following six steps:

Step 1. To learn how the two main financial statements of any business (balance sheet and P&L) are prepared and used.

Step 2. To introduce ratios and proportions and show how easily they can be developed and used.

Step 3. To explain different ratios and then provide examples that show how to get more meaning from your balance sheet and profit and loss account.

Step 4. To learn how to perform a ratio analysis. During this step you will learn how to collect data and compare your ratios with those of competitors.

Step 5. To understand how to examine expenses logically. This is important because if price or sales volume can't be raised, lowering expenses may be the answer to success or survival.

Step 6. To learn several proven ways of controlling your business – ie projecting how much cash you will need, when you need it, having enough cash for expansion, and for a new product introduction or sale.

How to Understand Financial Statements will teach you some of the basics, but will not make you an expert. It will help to clear up some misunderstandings about finance but will not turn you into an accountant. It simply gives you some tools that will help you control and predict the future of your business.

CHAPTER 1
Learning the Basics

Minimum competency

It is a demonstrable fact that the stagnation or failure of a business is often a result of over-buying, over-trading, or over-expanding. For example, a timber yard had a significant increase in sales for three years in a row and then failed. Why? Because the owner couldn't resist a bargain. He over-bought too much of too many items that were offered with bulk discounts. He used up so much cash that his ongoing expenses, such as rent, utilities and salaries, couldn't be paid on time.

Similarly, a plastics manufacturer had a modern, labour-saving plant, was well-stocked and had increasing sales. But this same manufacturer had to let go of some equity because a current loan couldn't be paid. Why? Because sales were obtained by offering loose credit terms and discounts. The results were that no cash was available to pay current debts.

Another new company developed a new product that quickly became sought-after. It was so much in demand that the company borrowed heavily to build a new plant and production line. It accepted more orders than could be reasonably fulfilled in the required amount of time and ended up delivering products very late. By the time the new plant was ready, demand had diminished and many of the old orders had been cancelled. Unfortunately, the debt had not. What happened? The business was sold to pay the debt. The business had over-expanded because it did not practice proper financial analysis.

The difference between failure and success is *not* always a lack of product knowledge or failing to put in long hours. More often it is not understanding the financial situation. Because new businesses usually have financial reports like a balance sheet and a profit and loss account prepared by someone in the family or by an accountant, owners or managers often do not understand the financial implications of their decisions and thus make poor choices.

To achieve a minimum competency in finance it is essential to understand balance sheets and profit and loss accounts thoroughly. This is what will be looked at next.

The anatomy of a balance sheet

The typical balance sheet displays the figures in vertical columns. Imagine that the 'balance' is achieved by having the business's assets on the right side of the page and liabilities and net worth on the left side like this:

BALANCE SHEET	
LIABILITIES **+** **NET WORTH**	**= ASSETS**

Assets are normally broken down into two main categories: current assets and fixed assets. Current assets usually mean anything that can be converted into cash within one year. Fixed assets are more permanent items like buildings or large pieces of equipment.

Liabilities are similarly divided. They are normally shown as current liabilities (that which is owed within one year) and long-term debt. Current liabilities include bills for items such as stock, salaries, rent, etc. Debt is normally items that by agreement need not be paid back quickly, such as a mortgage or long-term loan.

The *difference* between assets and liabilities equals net worth. That is, after all bills and loans are paid, anything left is called net worth. Another definition is that net worth is what is due the owner(s) of the business once all liabilities have been paid.

$$\text{ASSETS} - \text{LIABILITIES} = \text{NET WORTH}$$

OR

$$\text{ASSETS} = \text{LIABILITIES} + \text{NET WORTH}$$

Why is it called a 'balance sheet'?
The key word is *balance*. Because both the total assets and the liabilities and net worth totals are the same; they balance. This is true even if liabilities exceed the assets. In this case, net worth becomes negative and it must be subtracted from the liabilities, instead of being added.

How a balance sheet is prepared

A balance sheet is a document that uses the principle of double-entry accounting. It is called double entry because each business action affects two or more accounts. For example a sale will increase cash or debtors but decrease stocks. An account can be cash, stock, money you owe (creditors), or money owed to you (debtors) etc. Accounts are organised in categories called current or fixed assets on one side of the sheet, and current or long-term liabilities on the other. Assets and liabilities (plus net worth) must always balance (hence the name "balance sheet"). A glossary of basic terms is provided on page 20 for easy reference.

Let's suppose that a new business was started with the owner's savings of £100,000. The opening balance sheet would look something like this:

LIABILITIES	ASSETS
NET WORTH £100,000	CURRENT ASSETS Cash £100,000

The owner then decides to stock her shop and purchases £50,000 of merchandise (*stock*). She pays only £25,000 in cash (this will reduce *Cash* by £25,000) and promises to pay the other £25,000 in 30 days (this creates a new account called *Creditors*), that sum being placed under the category of *Current Liabilities*.

15

LIABILITIES		ASSETS	
CURRENT LIABILITIES		CURRENT ASSETS	
Creditors	£ 25,000	Cash	£ 75,000
NET WORTH	£100,000	**Stock**	**£ 50,000**
TOTAL	£125,000	TOTAL	£125,000

The balance sheet is in balance with the addition of £25,000 that is owed to the supplier. It is placed under current liabilities because it is due to be paid in a specified period which is less than one year. Current assets are those items that can be converted into cash within a year.

Now let's suppose that the owner buys a building for £100,000. She puts £25,000 down and obtains a £75,000 mortgage for the remainder.

The balance sheet would now look as shown opposite. (Note the addition of two new accounts, one called *Long-term Debt*, because it is to be paid over a period longer than a year, and the second called *Fixed Assets* which includes land, buildings and equipment.)

BALANCE SHEET

	£	£
CURRENT ASSETS		
Cash	50,000	
Stock	50,000	
TOTAL CURRENT ASSETS		100,000
FIXED ASSETS		
Building	**100,000**	
TOTAL FIXED ASSETS		100,000
TOTAL		£200,000
CURRENT LIABILITIES		
Creditors	25,000	
TOTAL CURRENT LIABILITIES		25,000
LONG TERM-DEBT		
Mortgage	**75,000**	
TOTAL LONG-TERM DEBT		75,000
NET WORTH		100,000
TOTAL		£200,000

When sales are made stock will decrease and cash will increase. If some sales are made on credit, a new account called Debtors will need to be added under current assets. Let's suppose that £20,000 of stock is sold for £25,000 (£15,000 is received as cash and £10,000 is on credit).

The balance sheet would look like this:

XXX COMPANY
BALANCE SHEET
YEAR END 19XX

	£	£
CURRENT ASSETS		
Cash	65,000	
Debtors	10,000	
Stock	30,000	
TOTAL CURRENT ASSETS		105,000
FIXED ASSETS		
Building	100,000	
TOTAL FIXED ASSETS		100,000
TOTAL		£205,000
CURRENT LIABILITIES		
Creditors	25,000	
TOTAL CURRENT LIABILITIES		25,000
LONG-TERM DEBT		
Mortgage	75,000	
TOTAL LONG-TERM DEBT		75,000
NET WORTH (OPENING)		100,000
GROSS PROFIT*	5,000	
NET WORTH (CLOSING)		105,000
TOTAL		£205,000

(*Profit from example sale)

Note that this business action affected three accounts which are on the asset side of the balance sheet, one account (Stock) lowered, the cash account increased and a new account called Debtors was added, so the total did not change.

To complete the balance sheet the company name and address has been added along with the date of preparation. The balance sheet is a snapshot of how a business stands *at any given point in time*.

Now let's see how the profit and loss account is prepared.

The anatomy of a profit and loss account

The profit and loss account shows all the actions of a business over a *period of time*: a month, a quarter or a year.

The profit and loss account, or P & L, is sometimes called an income statement. It begins when a sale is made. So the *first entry* or account would be *Sales*. This is how the £25,000 in sales would look on the profit and loss account:

Sales	£25,000

The next entry would be *cost of those goods sold*. Let's say that the cost of goods sold was £20,000. Cost of goods is normally the manufacturing cost, freight from the supplier, royalties, etc. Cost of goods is subtracted from sales to show a *gross profit* of £5,000 (gross profit is the money left over before deducting expenses and tax).

The added entries would appear on the profit and loss account as shown below:

Sales	£25,000
Cost of goods sold	£20,000
Gross profit	£ 5,000

The next entries that go on a profit and loss account are the expenses connected with running a business. Expenses are either cash or accrued. In the example below, expenses totalling £1,640 are identified.

The profit and loss account would now look as follows. (Note that it has a heading and that it covers a *period of time*, in this case one month.)

PROFIT AND LOSS ACCOUNT
XXX COMPANY
JANUARY 19XX

	£	£
Sales		25,000
Cost of goods sold		20,000
Gross profit		5,000
EXPENSES:		
Owner's wages	500	
Salaries	900	
Delivery	50	
Bad debt	20	
Insurance	30	
Rates	10	
Interest	50	
Advertising	80	
Total expenses		£ 1,640
NET PROFIT (before tax)		£ 3,360

(The total expenses are subtracted from the Gross profit to give a Net profit before tax of £3,360.)

Glossary of balance sheet terms

The balance sheet that will be used as an example for the rest of this book is shown on page 22. The following are definitions of the terms used in the balance sheet.

Accruals. Items such as wages that are charged against current profits but not yet paid.

Assets. The cash, money owed to the company, merchandise, land, buildings, and equipment that a company owns or that has money value.

Cash. Money you have control of and access to.

Creditors. Sometimes called trade creditors, these are the total of all moneys owed by the company to a supplier or vendor for raw materials, products or merchandise that are to be used to make goods for sale or to be resold as received.

Current Assets. The sum of cash, notes, and debtors (less reserves for bad debts), advances on stocks, stocks, and any other item that can be converted into cash in a short time, ie usually less than a year.

Current Liabilities. The total of all moneys owed by the company that will be due within one year.

Debtors. The moneys owed to the company for merchandise, products or services sold or performed but not yet collected.

Fixed Assets. Land, buildings, building equipment, fixtures, machinery, tools, furniture, patterns and drawings, less salvage value and depreciation.

Liabilities. Everything that a company owes to a creditor; liabilities are the debts owed by the company to others. Liabilities are accounts such as: loans repayable, accounts payable, or accruals. There are two categories of liabilities, current liabilities and long-term liabilities, or as used in this book, long-term debt.

Long-term Debt. Sometimes called long-term liabilities, it is all the obligations such as mortgages, bonds, term loans, and any other moneys that become due more than one year from the date of the statement.

Mortgage. Legal charge over property to cover a debt.

Net Worth. What the owner(s) has represented on a balance sheet as the difference between all assets and all liabilities, in other words, the owner's equity.

Notes Payable. Money borrowed by the company that will be paid back within one year.

Stocks. For a manufacturing firm it is the sum of finished merchandise on hand, raw material, and work-in-process. For retailers and wholesalers, it is the stock of saleable goods on hand.

XYZ HARDWARE AND BUILDING SUPPLY
BALANCE SHEET
YEAR END 19XX

CURRENT ASSETS

CASH	£ 2,000	
DEBTORS	85,000	
STOCK	210,000	
TOTAL CURRENT ASSETS		297,000
LAND/BUILDINGS	50,000	
EQUIPMENT/FIXTURES	50,000	
TOTAL FIXED ASSETS		100,000
TOTAL ASSETS		£397,000

CURRENT LIABILITIES

NOTES PAYABLE	£ 18,000	
CREDITORS	205,000	
ACCRUALS	6,000	
TOTAL CURRENT LIABILITIES		229,000
MORTGAGE	25,000	
TOTAL LONG-TERM DEBT		25,000
NET WORTH		143,000
TOTAL LIABILITIES AND NET WORTH		£397,000

Glossary of profit and loss account terms

The profit and loss account that will be used as an example for the rest of this book is shown on page 23. The following are definitions of terms used in a profit and loss account.

Net Sales. The total value of all cash or credit sales less returns, allowances, discounts and rebates.

Cost of Goods Sold. For a retail or wholesale business it is the total price paid for the products sold plus the cost of having them delivered to the store during the accounting period.

For a manufacturing firm it is the opening stocks plus purchases, delivery costs, materials, labour, and overheads minus the closing stock.

Gross Profit. Profit before expenses and tax have been deducted.

Expenses. The cost of doing business. It includes such items as: wages, telephone, insurance, depreciation, interest, and advertising.

Net Profit. The amount left over after expenses including interest but before tax. (The term *net profit* as used in this book will always be profit before tax.)

PROFIT AND LOSS ACCOUNT

		£
NET SALES (LESS ALLOWANCES & DISCOUNTS)		700,000
COST OF GOODS SOLD		500,000
GROSS PROFIT		200,000
EXPENSES	£	
SALARIES (OWNERS)	74,000	
WAGES	65,000	
DELIVERY	7,000	
BAD DEBT	4,000	
TELEPHONE	2,000	
DEPRECIATION	4,000	
INSURANCE	7,000	
RATES	8,000	
INTEREST	8,700	
ADVERTISING	3,000	
MISCELLANEOUS	2,000	
TOTAL EXPENSES		184,700
NET PROFIT (before tax)		£ 15,300

A look ahead

To assess your basic financial understanding, five questions are listed below. These were designed to demonstrate that although the balance sheet and profit and loss account contain considerable information, these instruments are only the launching pad of financial analysis. As we will soon learn, basic financial information can be used to develop simple ratios that will help you understand and control a business. Looking at your expenses as percentages of sales can help you reduce your costs; and keeping track of selected ratios and percentages over a period of time will help you chart the future with confidence.

Try the following questions. Don't worry if you can't answer them or don't understand them at this stage. By the end of this book you will!

From the balance sheet and profit and loss account on pages 22 and 23 can you:

1. Observe that the owner can't pay current bills? (Hint: check the cash available.)
2. Calculate what the average collection period for Debtors is over 30 days? (This will be covered in detail in Chapter 3 under ratios.)
3. Tell that the owner's return on investment (ROI) is less than what most experts say is necessary for future growth? (This will be apparent when you get to profitability ratios in Chapter 3.)
4. Determine where the profit is, since there is only £2,000 in cash? (*Hint:* it may be uncollected.)
5. See that the net worth of the owner is mainly composed of fixed assets? (This is what would be left when all debts are paid.)

The balance sheet and profit and loss account alone do not provide sufficient financial information to operate a business properly. For instance, these documents cannot tell you how long debts have remained uncollected, what adding a new employee would do to cash flow, or how much money it takes to support a marketing plan.

The answer to these and other key questions comes from knowing how to use the information in a balance sheet and profit and loss account. This is what you will learn in the pages ahead.

CHAPTER 2

Using the Tools of the Trade

Understanding ratios and percentages

Be patient with this chapter as it is important. It may sound complex at first, but will become clearer as you use ratios.

Why ratio analysis?

Ratios are common. You use them every day. They provide a better understanding of a wide range of situations. For instance, the miles you get per gallon (MPG) of petrol or the unemployment rate presented as ratios are easier to grasp than the total number of unemployed people or the total number of gallons of petrol used. Ratios are used when we are trying to get the best price per ounce of food, when we compare batting averages of cricketers, or when we measure the cost of a building in pounds per square foot.

Ratios are an even more important tool when used to measure the progress of a business and to compare a business to its competitors.

How ratios are developed

Ratios are expressed by placing one number over another number.

For example: $\frac{50}{100}$ is a ratio. It means that 50 is to be divided by 100. The answer will be a percentage. In this case .50 or 50 per cent because 50 is half of 100.

The number on top of a formula represents the figure you are comparing to the bottom figure (which is called the base). For instance, if the 50 in the above ratio represents £50 of sales and 100 represents £100 of fixed assets (such as a piece of equipment or a fixture), you are able to compare the amount of sales generated by the fixed assets. In this example, the sales amount to half the value of the fixed assets, or a return on fixed assets of 50 per cent.

Another way to express this is to use proportions. This means that fixed assets to sales is in the proportion of 2 to 1.

If the numbers were reversed: $\frac{100}{50}$ then sales become £100 and fixed assets £50. In this case the fixed assets generated 200 per cent or twice their value. In other words, 50 can go into 100 twice. The proportion of fixed assets to sales is now 1 to 2. Ratios are used to indicate how your business is doing. They do not make decisions for you in themselves, but do provide information from which to make sound decisions. More than one ratio should be examined before a major decision is made, but more on this later. Now, let's explore percentages and ratios in more depth.

What ratios measure
Ratios measure *proportions*. In our example of $\frac{100}{50}$ above, we were able to determine what proportion one figure is of another. Ratios also measure *relationships*. They do this because they can translate assets – such as tools, stocks and liabilities, and liabilities such as creditors and loans – into common figures in pounds. By doing this it is easy to see valuable relationships between two seemingly unrelated items. Ratios also allow you to make comparisons between the periods. For example, a ratio lets you measure your stock turnover from one month to another, or from year to year.

The 10 per cent paradox
Suppose you are asked if you would be willing to take a chance on an event that would pay you £100,000. All you had to do was call 'heads or tails' on the toss of a coin. Probability laws tell you that you have a 50-50 chance of winning. But, suppose you have to risk £10,000 (10 per cent) to participate in

the tossing of the coin? You might hold back from putting £10,000 at risk even though the pay-off would be large. However, you might be willing to risk less to get less, ie 10 per cent of £1,000 or £100. In other words, even though the percentage did not change, spending a large amount of 'real' money would make the difference. Ratios and percentages, therefore, need to be kept in context as to what they represent.

Using ratios without fear

Think of a ratio as a friend when scrutinising your business. Ratios are simple to calculate, especially with a hand-held calculator, and easy to use. They provide a wealth of information that cannot be obtained anywhere else.

Ratios cannot take the place of experience or replace good management, but they will make good managers better. Ratios can help to point out areas that need more investigating or assist in developing future operating strategy.

You can quickly learn to use a number of ratios by following the steps outlined in this book. The 'fill-in-the-blank' forms presented later, will assist you in analysing any business. Going through the forms provided should allow you to understand basic ratios and be comfortable using them.

Basic rules for ratios

To ease you into the use of ratios, carefully review the following five basic rules:

1. To determine a percentage change, suppose your sales increased 25 per cent during the first month of the year and 37 per cent in the second month. It would be wrong to state that the second month's increase was 12 per cent. This is because both were taken from the same base period (in this case 100). Therefore this is a 12 percentage *points* increase. To determine the actual monthly increase, the 12 point increase of the second month should be divided by the new base period of 125 (the starting figure plus the first month's

increase) for a true monthly increase of 9.5 per cent.

2. When comparing a part to a whole, such as net profits to sales, the whole is always the base. That is:

$$\frac{\text{net profits}}{\text{sales}}$$

3. A percentage of something can *increase* by more than 100 per cent but cannot *decrease* by more than 100 per cent. Think of it like this: you can double your money (200 per cent) but can lose 100 per cent of it only once.

4. Ratios lose significance and accuracy when they become excessively detailed. This is important because it means that you don't need a lot of detailed data or figures to use ratio analysis. Analysis is often significant when used in general ways (ie with rough working figures.)

5. Remember that ratios will assist you in decision making not make the decisions for you.

Points to remember when using ratios

Maintain an objective approach. Don't use ratios to support predetermined conclusions. Use them to help you understand your business better.

Don't use the wrong figures. For instance when looking at a percentage change between two figures, such as in price from £2.00 to £3.00, the number you want to compare is the *difference* between the two pound figures which is £1.00. This difference figure (£1.00) is then divided by £2.00 for a percentage increase of 50 per cent. Don't divided £2.00 by £3.00 or vice versa.

Don't compare meaningless numbers. For example, don't compare expenses to fixed assets. This number is easy to calculate but has no meaning in the operation of a business.

Summary

- You have been introduced to ratio analysis and now know that ratios are expressed as a percentage or a proportion.

- You have discovered that ratios are developed by dividing the number you wish to compare by the base number.

- You have seen that you use ratios in many of your home and business transactions. These are developed in the same way as the ratios we will learn to use in this book.

- You have learned that ratios are expressed like this:*

$$\frac{50}{100} = 50 \text{ per cent or 1 to 2 (1:2) and}$$

$$\frac{100}{50} = 2 \text{ times or 2 to 1 (2:1)}$$

- You have discovered that ratios can be easy to develop and use and have noted a few basic rules and points that will help you to understand them better.

- Finally, we hope you know that ratios are a friend and can help you control your business.

Hint: If the top number is smaller than the bottom number, the ratio will be a percentage. If the top number is larger than the bottom number the ratio will be expressed as 'times'.

CHAPTER 3

Three Types of Ratio: Liquidity, Profitability and Efficiency

Introduction to ratios

This chapter presents and explains several common ratios that can be used to measure and control a business. You will not use every ratio that is presented, especially if you are in a service business. It is not necessary to memorise the ratios or their meanings as given in this chapter, because you can always return to this part of the book for reference.

The first set of ratios is called *liquidity ratios* because they measure the amount of cash available to cover expenses, both current and long term. These ratios are especially important in keeping a business alive. Not paying your bills due to a shortage of cash is the fastest way to go out of business. Lending institutions often don't want to lend money when it is actually needed. Make arrangements for credit in good time. The best time to do this is when your business liquidity looks very good. Make sure your credit agreement is always in writing!

The second set of ratios is called *profitability ratios.* These ratios measure and help control income. This is done through higher sales, larger margins, getting more from your expenses, and/or a combination of these methods.

The third set of ratios is called *efficiency ratios.* Efficiency ratios measure and help control the operation of the business. They add another dimension to help you increase income by assessing such important transactions as the use of credit, control of stock, and/or management of assets.

Glossary for ratio analysis

Accounts Receivable. Pounds'-worth of credit sales not yet collected.

Cost of Goods Sold. For a retail or wholesale business, it is the total price paid for the products sold plus the cost of having them delivered, during the accounting period.

For a manufacturing firm, it is the opening stock plus purchases, delivery costs, materials, labour, and overheads minus the closing stock.

Current Assets. The sum of cash and debtors (less reserves for bad debts), advances on stock, stock, and anything else that can be converted into cash in a short time, usually less than a year.

Current Liabilities. The total of all moneys owed by the company that will fall due within one year.

Earnings Before Interest and Taxes (EBIT). Net profit before all interest payments and tax.

Fixed Assets. Land, buildings, building equipment, fixtures, machinery, tools, furniture, patterns and drawings, less salvage value and depreciation.

Net Profit. The amount left over after expenses plus interest and tax. (The term net profit as used in this book will always be before tax.)

Net Worth. What the owner(s) have represented on a balance sheet as the difference between all assets and all liabilities.

Sales (or net sales). The total value of all sales less returns, allowances, discounts, and rebates.

Stocks. For a manufacturing firm it is the sum of finished merchandise on hand, raw material, and work in progress.

For retailers and wholesalers, it is the stock of saleable goods on hand.

Total Assets. The sum of all current and fixed assets.

Total Debt. The sum of all liabilities, both current and long term.

Working Capital. Current assets less current liabilities.

Ratio 1: Liquidity ratios

The following pages will present three useful liquidity ratios. They will be shown with a balance sheet and profit and loss account followed by an explanation of what the ratios mean and how to use them on the right-hand page.

To fit all the information on to the page, the following abbreviations have sometimes been used:

TOTAL CA = total current assets
EQUIP/FIX = equipment and fixtures
TOTAL CA AND FA = total current assets and fixed assets
TOTAL CL = total current liabilities
TOTAL LIABILITIES AND NW = total liabilities and net worth

Note: Each figure used to develop a ratio will be highlighted on the balance sheet or P & L account to show exactly where it came from by using a shaded area.

XYZ HARDWARE AND BUILDING SUPPLY
BALANCE SHEET
YEAR END 19XX

	£	£
CURRENT ASSETS		
CASH	2,000	
DEBTORS	85,000	
STOCK	210,000	
TOTAL CA		297,000
LAND/BUILDINGS	50,000	
EQUIP/FIX	50,000	
TOTAL FIXED ASSETS		100,000
TOTAL CA AND FA		£397,000
CURRENT LIABILITIES		
NOTES PAYABLE	18,000	
CREDITORS	205,000	
ACCRUALS	6,000	
TOTAL CL		229,000
MORTGAGE	25,000	
TOTAL LONG-TERM DEBT		25,000
NET WORTH		143,000
TOTAL LIABILITIES AND NW		£397,000

PROFIT AND LOSS ACCOUNT

		£
NET SALES (LESS ALLOWANCES & DISCOUNTS		700,000
COST OF GOODS SOLD		500,000
GROSS PROFIT		200,000

EXPENSES	£	
SALARY (OWNER)	74,000	
WAGES	65,000	
DELIVERY	7,000	
BAD DEBT	4,000	
TELEPHONE	2,000	
DEPRECIATION	4,000	
INSURANCE	7,000	
RATES	8,000	
INTEREST	8,700	
ADVERTISING	3,000	
MISCELLANEOUS	2,000	
TOTAL EXPENSES		184,700
NET PROFIT (before tax)		£ 15,300

RATIO: CURRENT RATIO

$$\frac{\text{CURRENT ASSETS}}{\text{CURRENT LIABILITIES}} \quad \frac{£297,000}{£229,000} = 1.3 \text{ times}$$

Current ratio

Measures. The ability to meet short-term obligations.

Generally accepted standard. Current assets should be twice or 200 per cent of current liabilities.

Low ratio. A company may not be able to pay off bills as rapidly as it should. It may be able to take advantage of cash discounts or other favourable terms. It may not be able to keep its suppliers happy and receive eager service. High stocks mean high accounts payable.

High ratio. Money that could be working for the business is tied up in government securities, cash savings, or other safe funds.

Remarks. The proper ratio depends on the type of business, the time in the business cycle, and the age of the business. You need to enquire about what is proper in your type of business.

Quick ratio. Another variation is the quick ratio (or acid test) which is the same as the current ratio except that it eliminates stock so that only cash and debtors are counted. Some analysts reduce debtors by 25 per cent before using this ratio. Whether you do or not depends on how much faith you have in your ability to collect your debts. The ratio looks like this:

$$\frac{\text{cash} + \text{debtors}}{\text{current liabilities}} \quad \text{or} \quad \frac{£87,000^*}{£229,000} \;=\; 38 \text{ per cent}$$

A safe margin would be at least 1.0 times. The example shown above is less than a half to one, and suggests some serious problems such as slow moving stock.

*Cash	£ 2,000
Debtors	£85,000
	£87,000

XYZ HARDWARE AND BUILDING SUPPLY
BALANCE SHEET
YEAR END 19XX

	£	£
CURRENT ASSETS		
CASH	2,000	
DEBTORS	85,000	
STOCK	210,000	
TOTAL CA		297,000
LAND/BUILDINGS	50,000	
EQUIP/FIX	50,000	
TOTAL FIXED ASSETS		100,000
TOTAL CA AND FA		£397,000
CURRENT LIABILITIES		
NOTES PAYABLE	18,000	
CREDITORS	205,000	
ACCRUALS	6,000	
TOTAL CL		229,000
MORTGAGE	25,000	
TOTAL LONG-TERM DEBT		25,000
NET WORTH		143,000
TOTAL LIABILITIES AND NW		£397,000

PROFIT AND LOSS ACCOUNT

		£
NET SALES (LESS ALLOWANCES & DISCOUNTS)		700,000
COST OF GOODS SOLD		500,000
GROSS PROFIT		200,000
EXPENSES	£	
SALARY (OWNER)	74,000	
WAGES	65,000	
DELIVERY	7,000	
BAD DEBT	4,000	
TELEPHONE	2,000	
DEPRECIATION	4,000	
INSURANCE	7,000	
RATES	8,000	
INTEREST	8,700	
ADVERTISING	3,000	
MISCELLANEOUS	2,000	
TOTAL EXPENSES		184,700
NET PROFIT (before tax)		£ 15,300

RATIO: TURNOVER OF CASH

$$\frac{\text{SALES}}{\text{WORKING CAPITAL}} \qquad \frac{£700,000}{£68,000^*} = 10.3 \text{ times}$$

*(Working capital = current assets − current liabilities) = £297,000 − £229,000 = £68,000

Turnover of cash ratio

> *Note:* It's called working capital because it is the amount necessary to operate your business on a daily basis. Working capital is the money you use for salaries, to pay your bills, etc. The amount of your working capital changes every time you receive cash, make a cash sale, or write a cheque.

Measures. The turnover of cash or working capital. Maintaining a positive cash flow or working capital balance will provide an adequate means of financing your sales without struggling to pay for the materials and/or goods you are buying.

Generally accepted standard. Sales should be five or six times working capital.

Low ratio. You may have funds tied up in short-term low-yielding assets. This means that you may be able to manage on less cash.

High ratio. A vulnerability to creditors, such as the inability to pay wages or utility bills.

Remarks. Usually, if the current assets/current liabilities ratio is low, the turnover of cash ratio will be high. This is due to the small amount of working capital that is available.

XYZ HARDWARE AND BUILDING SUPPLY
BALANCE SHEET
YEAR END 19XX

	£	£
CURRENT ASSETS		
CASH	2,000	
DEBTORS	85,000	
STOCK	210,000	
TOTAL CA		297,000
LAND/BUILDINGS	50,000	
EQUIP/FIX	50,000	
TOTAL FIXED ASSETS		100,000
TOTAL CA AND FA		£397,000
CURRENT LIABILITIES		
NOTES PAYABLE	18,000	
CREDITORS	205,000	
ACCRUALS	6,000	
TOTAL CL		229,000
MORTGAGE	25,000	PLUS
TOTAL LONG-TERM DEBT		25,000
NET WORTH		143,000
TOTAL LIABILITIES AND NW		£397,000

PROFIT AND LOSS ACCOUNT

	£
NET SALES (LESS ALLOWANCES & DISCOUNTS)	700,000
COST OF GOODS SOLD	500,000
GROSS PROFIT	200,000

EXPENSES	£	
SALARY (OWNER)	74,000	
WAGES	65,000	
DELIVERY	7,000	
BAD DEBT	4,000	
TELEPHONE	2,000	
DEPRECIATION	4,000	
INSURANCE	7,000	
RATES	8,000	
INTEREST	8,700	
ADVERTISING	3,000	
MISCELLANEOUS	2,000	
TOTAL EXPENSES		184,700
NET PROFIT (before tax)		£ 15,300

RATIO: DEBT TO NET WORTH

$$\frac{\text{TOTAL DEBT}}{\text{NET WORTH}} \quad \frac{£254,000 \, (£229,000 + £25,000)}{£143,000} = 1.8 \text{ times}$$

Debt to net worth ratio

Measures. Total debt coverage expresses the relationship between capital contributed by the creditors and that contributed by the owner(s).

Generally accepted standard. Current liabilities should not be less than 1.25 times net worth or the creditors may want as much say in the operation of your business as you. Some analysts feel that *current liabilities* to net worth shouldn't exceed 80 per cent and *long-term debt* should not exceed net worth by 50 per cent.

Low ratio. Greater long-term financial security. This would generally mean that you have greater flexibility to borrow money. An extremely low ratio may mean that the firm's management is too conservative. This may indicate the firm is not reaching its full profit potential — that is, the profit potential from *gearing*, which is realised by borrowing money at a low rate of interest and obtaining a higher rate of return on sales.

High ratio. Greater risk being assumed by the creditors, hence greater interest on their part in the way the firm is being managed. Your ability to obtain money from outside sources is limited.

Remarks. Again, a lot depends on where the business is in its life cycle, what the policies of the owners are, the state of the economy, and the particular business cycle. Remember long-term debt is gearing. Gearing can work for you during the good times and against you during a slump in sales. This can result in a fall in earnings if too much money is borrowed.

Summary of liquidity ratios

Having read this far, you are well on your way to mastering the use of ratio analysis.

- Liquidity ratios help you to determine your firm's ability to pay debts.

- The current ratio is important as it provides an indication of your ability to pay your immediate bills.

- Working capital is the difference between current assets and current liabilities. This is an important figure because it represents the amount available to pay for salaries or new materials or goods.

- By maintaining a proper ratio for your turnover of cash you will be able to take advantage of discounts for prompt payment.

- Your total debt should not exceed 80 per cent of your net worth and your long-term debt should not exceed 50 per cent of your net worth.

Ratio 2: Profitability ratios

Profitability is why most of us are in business. We want a better return on our money and time than we can get from a bank or other low-risk interest-paying opportunity. This, by the way, is one of the most commonly used methods to evaluate whether you are doing well with your business. For example, if savings accounts or money market accounts are paying a higher percentage than you are earning on the money you have invested in your business, you will probably want to consider selling your business and reinvesting your money elsewhere, unless you like your line of work better than making more money. Profitability ratios provide you with the means to measure your earnings in several ways (as we will soon see). They measure your profit margin, return on assets, return on investment, and return on sales.

As a general rule, profitability, or income as it is sometimes called, comes about from changes in price or volume or both. Therefore, changes of your ratios over a period of time will come about as a result of what you do that affects changes in your price and/or volume. This will show up as increases in expenses such as more sales people or advertising, as changes resulting from assets depreciating or new ones being added, or if borrowing takes place. If you raise or lower your prices, changes will usually be shown by changes in your ratios.

Abbreviations used on the balance sheet are:
TOTAL CA = total current assets; EQUIP/FIX = equipment and fixtures; TOTAL CA AND FA = total current assets and fixed assets; TOTAL CL = total current liabilities; TOTAL LIABILITIES AND NW = total liabilities and net worth.

Note: Each figure used to develop a ratio will be highlighted on the balance sheet or P & L account to show exactly where it came from by using a shaded area.

XYZ HARDWARE AND BUILDING SUPPLY
BALANCE SHEET
YEAR END 19XX

	£	£
CURRENT ASSETS		
CASH	2,000	
DEBTORS	85,000	
STOCK	210,000	
TOTAL CA		297,000
LAND/BUILDINGS	50,000	
EQUIP/FIX	50,000	
TOTAL FIXED ASSETS		100,000
TOTAL CA AND FA		£397,000
CURRENT LIABILITIES		
NOTES PAYABLE	18,000	
CREDITORS	205,000	
ACCRUALS	6,000	
TOTAL CL		229,000
MORTGAGE	25,000	
TOTAL LONG-TERM DEBT		25,000
NET WORTH		143,000
TOTAL LIABILITIES AND NW		£397,000

PROFIT AND LOSS ACCOUNT

		£
NET SALES (LESS ALLOWANCES & DISCOUNTS)		700,000
COST OF GOODS SOLD		500,000
GROSS PROFIT		200,000

EXPENSES	£	
SALARY (OWNER)	74,000	
WAGES	65,000	
DELIVERY	7,000	
BAD DEBT	4,000	
TELEPHONE	2,000	
DEPRECIATION	4,000	
INSURANCE	7,000	
RATES	8,000	
INTEREST	8,700	
ADVERTISING	3,000	PLUS
MISCELLANEOUS	2,000	
TOTAL EXPENSES		184,700
NET PROFIT (before tax)		£ 15,300

RATIO: NET PROFIT

$$\frac{EBIT^*}{NET\ SALES} \quad \frac{£24,000\ (£15,300 + £8,700)}{£700,000} = 3.4\%$$

*Earnings before interest and tax

Net profit ratio

Measures. The effectiveness of management. This is a valid comparison between firms in the same industry. This ratio filters any distortions that may occur because of high debt or other factors that may affect tax payments or lack of tax payments.

Generally accepted standards. Depends on the business and/or industry. The volume of business is also an important factor as well as the age of your business.

Low ratio. Perhaps the expenses of doing business are too great; there are inefficiencies; or sales are too low for the costs.

High ratio. There is a high earnings margin or expenses are being held down.

Remarks. The measure of what is a good ratio is dependent on the type of business or industry. This should be compared to the industry standards. Earnings before interest and tax (EBIT) are also called operating income.

This ratio does not consider any investment made in buildings, machinery, etc. The investment turnover ratio on page 69 considers these types of capital investments, but it does not consider expenses.

XYZ HARDWARE AND BUILDING SUPPLY
BALANCE SHEET
YEAR END 19XX

	£	£
CURRENT ASSETS		
CASH	2,000	
DEBTORS	85,000	
STOCK	210,000	
TOTAL CA		297,000
LAND/BUILDINGS	50,000	
EQUIP/FIX	50,000	
TOTAL FIXED ASSETS		100,000
TOTAL CA AND FA		£397,000
CURRENT LIABILITIES		
NOTES PAYABLE	18,000	
CREDITORS	205,000	
ACCRUALS	6,000	
TOTAL CL		229,000
MORTGAGE	25,000	
TOTAL LONG-TERM DEBT		25,000
NET WORTH		143,000
TOTAL LIABILITIES AND NW		£397,000

PROFIT AND LOSS ACCOUNT

		£
NET SALES (LESS ALLOWANCES & DISCOUNTS)		700,000
COST OF GOODS SOLD		500,000
GROSS PROFIT		200,000

EXPENSES	£	
SALARY (OWNER)	74,000	
WAGES	65,000	
DELIVERY	7,000	
BAD DEBT	4,000	
TELEPHONE	2,000	
DEPRECIATION	4,000	
INSURANCE	7,000	
RATES	8,000	
INTEREST	8,700	
ADVERTISING	3,000	
MISCELLANEOUS	2,000	
TOTAL EXPENSES		184,700
NET PROFIT (before tax)		£ 15,300

RATIO: RATE OF RETURN ON SALES

$$\frac{\text{NET PROFIT}}{\text{NET SALES}} \quad \frac{£15,300}{£700,000} \quad = \quad 2.2\%$$

NUJ Ratio.

49

Rate of return on sales ratio

Measures. How much net profit was derived from every pound of sales. It indicates how well you have managed your operating expenses. It may also indicate whether the business is generating enough sales to cover the fixed costs and still leave an acceptable profit.

Generally accepted standard. Depends on the business and/ or the industry. Price and volume are important and play a large role in determining this ratio.

Low ratio. May not mean too much in some industries; for instance, a business that has a high stock turnover or one that uses low margins to attract business, such as a grocery shop, might show a low ratio but still be healthy.

High ratio. Usually the higher the ratio the better. However, if you are ahead of last year's figures and showing a steady increase, you are on the right track.

Remarks. In analysing your business, this ratio must be viewed bearing many facts in mind and used in conjunction with other ratios and analytical tools. Beware of using this ratio alone as you can easily end up comparing apples and oranges. Comparing it with your own results month after month, or year after year, is worth while.

XYZ HARDWARE AND BUILDING SUPPLY
BALANCE SHEET
YEAR END 19XX

	£	£
CURRENT ASSETS		
CASH	2,000	
DEBTORS	85,000	
STOCK	210,000	
TOTAL CA		297,000
LAND/BUILDINGS	50,000	
EQUIP/FIX	50,000	
TOTAL FIXED ASSETS		100,000
TOTAL CA AND FA		£397,000
CURRENT LIABILITIES		
NOTES PAYABLE	18,000	
CREDITORS	205,000	
ACCRUALS	6,000	
TOTAL CL		229,000
MORTGAGE	25,000	
TOTAL LONG-TERM DEBT		25,000
NET WORTH		143,000
TOTAL LIABILITIES AND NW		£397,000

PROFIT AND LOSS ACCOUNT

		£
NET SALES (LESS ALLOWANCES & DISCOUNTS)		700,000
COST OF GOODS SOLD		500,000
GROSS PROFIT		200,000

EXPENSES	£	
SALARY (OWNER)	74,000	
WAGES	65,000	
DELIVERY	7,000	
BAD DEBT	4,000	
TELEPHONE	2,000	
DEPRECIATION	4,000	
INSURANCE	7,000	
RATES	8,000	
INTEREST	8,700	
ADVERTISING	3,000	
MISCELLANEOUS	2,000	
TOTAL EXPENSES		184,700
NET PROFIT (before tax)		£ 15,300

RATIO: RETURN ON INVESTMENT (ROI)

$$\frac{\text{NET PROFIT}}{\text{NET SALES}} \quad \frac{£15,300}{£143,000} = 10.7\%$$

equity   worth
        Assets - liabilities

Return on investment ratio (ROI)

Measures. Return on the owner's investment (ROI). Some use this figure as a final evaluation.

Generally accepted standard. A relationship of at least 20 per cent is generally considered necessary to fund future growth.

Low ratio. Perhaps you could have done better investing your money in savings bonds or some other investment opportunity. This could indicate inefficient management performance or it could reflect a highly capitalised conservatively operated business.

High ratio. Perhaps creditors were a source of much of the funds, or management is efficient, or the firm is under-capitalised.

Remarks. This measure is considered one of the best criteria of profitability; it can be a key ratio to compare against other firms or the industry average. However, it should be used in conjunction with other ratios. There should be a direct relationship between ROI and risk; that is, the greater the risk, the higher the return. Remember, net worth is the difference between assets and liabilities. A smaller net worth figure would equate to a higher ratio.

Another measure of ROI is:

$$\frac{EBIT^*}{NET\ WORTH} = \frac{24,000}{143,000} = 16.7\ per\ cent$$

Note. The above is a combination of the profitability ratio called *net profit* (page 47) and the efficiency ratio called *investment turnover*, (page 69). This ratio overcomes the shortcomings of both. But make sure you look at each separately to discover what might have caused any changes: increased income from more sales or better use of your assets.

*EBIT = earnings before interest and tax

XYZ HARDWARE AND BUILDING SUPPLY
BALANCE SHEET
YEAR END 19XX

	£	£
CURRENT ASSETS		
CASH	2,000	
DEBTORS	85,000	
STOCK	210,000	
TOTAL CA		297,000
LAND/BUILDINGS	50,000	
EQUIP/FIX	50,000	
TOTAL FIXED ASSETS		100,000
TOTAL CA AND FA		£397,000
CURRENT LIABILITIES		
NOTES PAYABLE	18,000	
CREDITORS	205,000	
ACCRUALS	6,000	
TOTAL CL		229,000
MORTGAGE	25,000	
TOTAL LONG-TERM DEBT		25,000
NET WORTH		143,000
TOTAL LIABILITIES AND NW		£397,000

PROFIT AND LOSS ACCOUNT

		£
NET SALES (LESS ALLOWANCES & DISCOUNTS)		700,000
COST OF GOODS SOLD		500,000
GROSS PROFIT		200,000

EXPENSES	£	
SALARY (OWNER)	74,000	
WAGES	65,000	
DELIVERY	7,000	
BAD DEBT	4,000	
TELEPHONE	2,000	
DEPRECIATION	4,000	
INSURANCE	7,000	
RATES	8,000	
INTEREST	8,700	
ADVERTISING	3,000	
MISCELLANEOUS	2,000	
TOTAL EXPENSES		184,700
NET PROFIT (before tax)		£ 15,300

RATIO: RATE OF RETURN ON ASSETS

$$\frac{\text{NET PROFIT}}{\text{TOTAL ASSETS}} \quad \frac{£15,300}{£397,000} \quad = \quad 3.8\%$$

Inventory Turnover.

Rate of return on assets ratio

Measures. The profit that is generated by the use of the assets of the business.

Generally accepted standard. Varies a great deal depending on the industry and the amount of fixed assets that must be used, the amount of cash that must be available, etc.

Low ratio. Poor performance, or ineffective employment of the assets by management.

High ratio. Good performance, or effective use of the firm's assets by management.

Remarks. This ratio can easily be distorted by a heavily depreciated plant, a large amount of intangible assets, or unusual income or expense items. This ratio should be used with other ratios to compare firms in the same industry and of approximately the same size. It is a valid tool if you know the real value of your competitor's assets (especially fixed assets) and whether they are including outside earnings as a large part of their current assets. If you don't know, beware of coming to a firm conclusion from this ratio alone.

A variation of this ratio would be to split the assets into fixed and current and to work out a ratio for each of them. Knowing the return on fixed assets could be important to a business that has to count on a heavy investment in fixed assets, such as rolling stock or heavy machinery, to generate sales and profits.

Summary of profitability ratios

- Profitability ratios measure profit margin, return on assets, return on investment, and return on sales.
- Profitability is a result of several things such as: your price structure, the amount of business you do, and how well you control your expenses.
- The net profit ratio is a valid ratio to compare your business to your industry average.
- Your return on investment can be compared as a return on net worth or total assets.
- The rate of return on sales must be used with caution when comparing your business with others.

- Beware of using the rate of return on total assets to compare your business with others without knowing the following: the condition of the fixed assets; if the fixed assets are leased; and if outside earnings are a part of current assets.

Ratio 3: Efficiency ratios

Efficiency ratios measure how well you are conducting your business. These ratios provide an indication of how fast you are collecting your money for credit sales and how many times you are turning over your stock in a given period of time. They measure the amount of sales generated by your assets and the return you are earning on your assets.

Efficiency ratios are an important landmark when it comes to keeping your business in balance. For instance, if you start to offer credit too freely in order to generate sales, this will show up as an increase in the average number of days it takes to collect your debtors. If you over-buy, even with the best intentions of not passing up a real bargain, this will be reflected in a decrease in the turnover of your stock. Similarly, if you acquire too many fixed assets without a corresponding increase in sales, this ratio will quickly let you know that less sales are being generated by your assets.

Of course, other ratios will also play a part in maintaining the balance in your business that will lead to healthy growth, but the efficiency ratios will usually highlight your position sooner. You will notice that some efficiency ratios are in days rather than percentages or proportions.

Abbreviations used on the balance sheet are: TOTAL CA = total current assets; EQUIP/FIX = equipment and fixtures; TOTAL CA AND FA = total current assets and fixed assets; TOTAL CL = total current liabilities; TOTAL LIABILITIES AND NW = total liabilities and net worth.

XYZ HARDWARE AND BUILDING SUPPLY
BALANCE SHEET
YEAR END 19XX

	£	£
CURRENT ASSETS		
CASH	2,000	
DEBTORS	85,000	
STOCK	210,000	
TOTAL CA		297,000
LAND/BUILDINGS	50,000	
EQUIP/FIX	50,000	
TOTAL FIXED ASSETS		100,000
TOTAL CA AND FA		£397,000
CURRENT LIABILITIES		
NOTES PAYABLE	18,000	
CREDITORS	205,000	
ACCRUALS	6,000	
TOTAL CL		229,000
MORTGAGE	25,000	
TOTAL LONG-TERM DEBT		25,000
NET WORTH		143,000
TOTAL LIABILITIES AND NW		£397,000

PROFIT AND LOSS ACCOUNT

	£
NET SALES (LESS ALLOWANCES & DISCOUNTS)	700,000
COST OF GOODS SOLD	500,000
GROSS PROFIT	200,000

EXPENSES	£
SALARY (OWNER)	74,000
WAGES	65,000
DELIVERY	7,000
BAD DEBT	4,000
TELEPHONE	2,000
DEPRECIATION	4,000
INSURANCE	7,000
RATES	8,000
INTEREST	8,700
ADVERTISING	3,000
MISCELLANEOUS	2,000

TOTAL EXPENSES	184,700
NET PROFIT (before tax)	£ 15,300

RATIO: AVERAGE COLLECTION PERIOD FOR DEBTORS

$$\frac{\text{DEBTORS} \times 365 \text{ DAYS/YEAR}}{\text{SALES}} \quad \frac{£85,000 \times 365}{£700,000^*} = 44 \text{ DAYS}$$

Note: For convenience, it has been assumed that all sales were credit sales.

Average collection period ratio

Measures. The turnover of debtors — the average period it takes to collect payment for your credit sales.

Generally accepted standard. Depends on your collection period policy . . . if it is 30 days, then 30 days is the standard.

High ratio. A slow turnover — which may be the result of a number of bad accounts, or a lax collection policy, or perhaps increased credit is being used to generate sales.

Low ratio. A fast turnover — which could be the result of a stringent collection policy or fast-paying customers.

Remarks. Generally anything within 10–15 days of *your* collection period is deemed acceptable and considered within the collection period.

Note. Another variation is shown below. It is a two-step process that first measures your average daily credit sales and then provides the average collection period. If average daily credit sales are important, then use this ratio — if not, the other is easier and quicker to use. Both provide the same answer.

$$\frac{\text{Net credit sales}}{365} = \frac{700{,}000}{365} = £1{,}918 = \textbf{Daily credit sales}$$

$$\frac{\text{Debtors}}{\textbf{Daily credit sales}} = \frac{85{,}000}{1{,}918} = 44 \text{ days} = \text{Average collection period}$$

XYZ HARDWARE AND BUILDING SUPPLY
BALANCE SHEET
YEAR END 19XX

	£	£
CURRENT ASSETS		
CASH	2,000	
DEBTORS	85,000	
STOCK	210,000	
TOTAL CA		297,000
LAND/BUILDINGS	50,000	
EQUIP/FIX	50,000	
TOTAL FIXED ASSETS		100,000
TOTAL CA AND FA		£397,000
CURRENT LIABILITIES		
NOTES PAYABLE	18,000	
CREDITORS	205,000	
ACCRUALS	6,000	
TOTAL CL		229,000
MORTGAGE	25,000	
TOTAL LONG-TERM DEBT		25,000
NET WORTH		143,000
TOTAL LIABILITIES AND NW		£397,000

PROFIT AND LOSS ACCOUNT

	£
NET SALES (LESS ALLOWANCES & DISCOUNTS)	700,000
COST OF GOODS SOLD	500,000
Gross profit	200,000

EXPENSES	£	
SALARY (OWNER)	74,000	
WAGES	65,000	
DELIVERY	7,000	
BAD DEBT	4,000	
TELEPHONE	2,000	
DEPRECIATION	4,000	
INSURANCE	7,000	
RATES	8,000	
INTEREST	8,700	
ADVERTISING	3,000	
MISCELLANEOUS	2,000	
TOTAL EXPENSES		184,700
NET PROFIT (before tax)		£ 15,300

RATIO: STOCK TURNOVER — ALSO CALLED THE STOCK TO SALES RATIO

$$\frac{\text{COST-OF-GOODS-SOLD}}{\text{AVERAGE STOCK}} \quad \frac{£500,000}{£210,000} = 2.4 \text{ TIMES (152 DOH)*}$$

OR

$$\frac{\text{NET SALES}}{\text{AVERAGE STOCK}} \quad \frac{£700,000}{£210,000} = 3.3 \text{ TIMES (110 DOH)*}$$

*DOH = days on hand, see remarks on opposite page.

The cost-of-goods-sold figure is used by some analysts because most stocks are carried on the balance sheet by how much they cost, not the selling price, which is shown by using net sales.

Stock turnover ratio

> *Note*. Manufacturers' stock = finished goods, raw materials, and work-in-progress.
>
> Retailers'/wholesalers' stock = saleable goods on hand.

Measures. Stock turnover. This shows how fast your merchandise is moving. That is, how many times your initial stock is replaced in a month/year.

Generally accepted standard. Depends on the industry and even the time of year for some industries. However, six to seven times is a rule of thumb.

Low ratio. An indication of a large stock, a never-out-of-stock situation, perhaps some obsolete items, or maybe an indication of poor liquidity, some possible overstocking of items, or a planned build-up in anticipation of an approaching high-selling period.

High ratio. An indication of a narrow selection, maybe fast-moving merchandise, or perhaps some lost sales. It may indicate better liquidity, perhaps superior merchandising, or a shortage of stock needed for sales.

Remarks. Faster turnovers are generally viewed as a positive trend; they increase cash flow, reduce warehousing, etc. This ratio measures how management is using stock and can be used to compare one period to the next or one company to another in the same industry or to the industry average. Again, it is an indicator, rather than an absolute measure-ment or count. As a general rule, a small retail business should not carry more than 100 per cent of its working capital in stock.

> *Note*.
> **DOH:** Another measurement is to take the stock turnover (ST) ratio and divide it into 365 days:
>
> $\dfrac{365}{ST}$ = the average number of days the stock is on hand.
>
> $\dfrac{365}{2.4}$ = 152 days on hand.

XYZ HARDWARE AND BUILDING SUPPLY
BALANCE SHEET
YEAR END 19XX

	£	£
CURRENT ASSETS		
CASH	2,000	
DEBTORS	85,000	
STOCK	210,000	
TOTAL CA		297,000
LAND/BUILDINGS	50,000	
EQUIP/FIX	50,000	
TOTAL FIXED ASSETS		100,000
TOTAL CA AND FA		£397,000
CURRENT LIABILITIES		
NOTES PAYABLE	18,000	
CREDITORS	205,000	
ACCRUALS	6,000	
TOTAL CL		229,000
MORTGAGE	25,000	
TOTAL LONG-TERM DEBT		25,000
NET WORTH		143,000
TOTAL LIABILITIES AND NW		£397,000

PROFIT AND LOSS ACCOUNT

	£
NET SALES (LESS ALLOWANCES & DISCOUNTS)	700,000
COST OF GOODS SOLD	500,000
GROSS PROFIT	200,000

EXPENSES	£	
SALARY (OWNER)	74,000	
WAGES	65,000	
DELIVERY	7,000	
BAD DEBT	4,000	
TELEPHONE	2,000	
DEPRECIATION	4,000	
INSURANCE	7,000	
RATES	8,000	
INTEREST	8,700	
ADVERTISING	3,000	
MISCELLANEOUS	2,000	
TOTAL EXPENSES		184,700
NET PROFIT (before tax)		£ 15,300

RATIO: FIXED ASSETS: NET WORTH

$$\frac{\text{FIXED ASSETS}}{\text{NET WORTH}} \quad \frac{£100,000}{£143,000} = 70\%$$

Fixed assets to net worth ratio

Measures. The amount of fixed assets that are a part of net worth. This ratio is important because it provides an indication of how much capital is tied up in low-liquid assets.

Generally accepted standard. A rule of thumb for small business is that not more than 75 per cent of your net worth should be tied up in fixed assets. If fixed assets are approaching 75 per cent of the firm's net worth, the firm may find it difficult to make working capital meet current expenses.

Low ratio. A proportionately smaller investment is fixed assets in relation to net worth, that is, net worth may consist of more liquid-type assets. This is a better situation for the creditors.

High ratio. A larger investment in plant and property, which may be hard to liquidate if cash is needed, especially if they are not paid for.

Remarks. Fixed assets are carried on the balance sheet as depreciated fixed assets, not original cost. The presence of substantial leased fixed assets (those not shown on a balance sheet) may deceptively lower this ratio. The amount of fixed assets depends on the industry: for example, the fixed asset requirement for a haulage company or a heavy equipment operating business may be relatively high, but it will be low for an average retailer or consultant and not of such significance.

XYZ HARDWARE AND BUILDING SUPPLY
BALANCE SHEET
YEAR END 19XX

	£	£
CURRENT ASSETS		
CASH	2,000	
DEBTORS	85,000	
STOCK	210,000	
TOTAL CA		297,000
LAND/BUILDINGS	50,000	
EQUIP/FIX	50,000	
TOTAL FIXED ASSETS		100,000
TOTAL CA AND FA		£397,000
CURRENT LIABILITIES		
NOTES PAYABLE	18,000	
CREDITORS	205,000	
ACCRUALS	6,000	
TOTAL CL		229,000
MORTGAGE	25,000	
TOTAL LONG-TERM DEBT		25,000
NET WORTH		143,000
TOTAL LIABILITIES AND NW		£397,000

PROFIT AND LOSS ACCOUNT

	£
NET SALES (LESS ALLOWANCES & DISCOUNTS)	700,000
COST OF GOODS SOLD	500,000
GROSS PROFIT	200,000

EXPENSES	£	
SALARY (OWNER)	74,000	
WAGES	65,000	
DELIVERY	7,000	
BAD DEBT	4,000	
TELEPHONE	2,000	
DEPRECIATION	4,000	
INSURANCE	7,000	
RATES	8,000	
INTEREST	8,700	
ADVERTISING	3,000	
MISCELLANEOUS	2,000	
TOTAL EXPENSES		184,700
NET PROFIT (before tax)		£ 15,300

RATIO: INVESTMENT TURNOVER

$$\frac{\text{NET SALES}}{\text{TOTAL ASSETS}} \quad \frac{£700,000}{£397,000} \quad = \quad 1.8 \text{ times}$$

Investment turnover ratio

Measures. Ability of the firm to generate sales in relation to assets.

Generally accepted standard. This will vary greatly depending on the business and the industry; for instance a service business would have limited fixed assets and little if any stock compared to a manufacturing company.

Low ratio. The assets may not be fully employed or too many assets may be chasing too few sales. The assets are not pulling their own weight. The firm may be expanding but the business is not growing.

High ratio. More sales may be generated with fewer assets. This may indicate that something is going or has gone well. Maybe you are getting more sales from the same level of buildings and equipment.

Remarks. This ratio should be used only to compare firms within specific industry groups and in conjunction with other ratios. As with any ratio measuring assets, it can give a distorted reading if the assets are heavily depreciated or if there is a large amount of intangible assets, such as goodwill. Be careful when comparing two firms or comparing with the industry averages that the asset figures are approximately the same. This ratio does not consider a price increase or decrease or how well you watch your expenses. This ratio, when combined with the net profit ratio on page 47, becomes another return on investment (ROI) ratio. See page 53.

Another version is:

$$\frac{\text{Net sales}}{\text{Fixed assets}} = \frac{£700,000}{£100,000} = 7 \text{ times}$$

This is important if your business requires a large investment in fixed assets.

Summary of efficiency ratios

- Efficiency ratios measure how well you are conducting your business.

- Efficiency ratios help to keep your business in balance.

- Your debtors, times 365 days, divided by your credit sales will tell you the length of time it takes your average customer to pay his or her bills.

- Dividing the cost of goods sold by your average stock will provide you with the number of times you replace your stock per month or per year.

- To find out the amount of fixed assets that are a part of your net worth divide your fixed assets by your net worth.

- Your net sales divided by your total assets will tell you how well you are generating sales in relation to your total assets.

- A variation of the above ratio is to substitute fixed assets for total assets to see how well you are generating sales in relation to your fixed assets.

CHAPTER 4

How to Perform a Ratio Analysis

Introduction

Now that you have learned what ratios are and what they can do for you, we are ready to organise and use ratios in analysing a business. This chapter will provide forms and charts that will help you to collect, organise, and evaluate your business through the use of a ratio review chart.

Data collection charts

The two forms on pages 75 and 76 will help you to organise your ratios and assist you in using your *ratio review chart*. The first form is the *data gathering form*. It provides a means of gathering the necessary figures from the balance sheet and profit and loss account.

The second form is the *comparison chart*. This provides spaces so that you can work out your ratios and insert your industry averages. Industry average figures are compiled by several sources. This information may be purchased, but it is usually available through a bank, library or Chamber of Commerce. Your trade association may also compile similar statistics both nationally and regionally. Regional numbers may be more appropriate for your use. To make the best use of these forms, fill in the blanks from your balance sheet and profit and loss account. Examples of completed forms are shown on pages 73 and 74. These samples are based on the same balance sheet and profit and loss account we have been using.

What is significant?

To determine which ratios to use, consider what type of business you have, the age of your business, where you are in the business cycle, and what you are looking for. For instance, one type of business might require a large number of fixed assets, buildings, land, equipment, tools, etc, while another requires very few. The significant ratios in the first case would be those that help you to measure how well you are using your fixed assets.

Another type of business may need to carry high stocks or alternatively just enough to satisfy emergency needs. In either case, stock turnover is critical and if it gets out of hand you may be unable to pay current expenses on the one hand, or lack the stock to satisfy your customers on the other.

The age of your business is important. If you have passed the initial three to five years start-up period and have liquidity, you are probably interested in expansion. In this case, the profitability and efficiency ratios will be factors you need to monitor closely. Be careful to keep your business operations in balance.

Some businesses are dependent upon the seasons for their income. That is, more sales occur during certain periods of the year than any other. During each rise and fall of this seasonal pattern, ratios can be quite different. It becomes necessary to watch these periods so that your ratios reflect what is needed. For example, if you are expecting a big sale but it hasn't come through, or are anticipating a low sales period, you will need liquidity to carry you through. If you sell on credit, you will need to keep your eye on your collection time between the sale and the payment, or you could face a lack of working capital.

Finally, if you are planning to expand, you should be able to show regular profits which are in line with your industry. A low debt structure will also help to influence lenders to provide the money you need at a favourable interest rate.

DATA GATHERING FORM

BUSINESS NAME: **XYZ Hardware and Building Supply**
BUSINESS ADDRESS: **Anywhere, UK**

DATE PREPARED: **date/month/year**

ITEMS	£ FIGURES
CURRENT ASSETS	£297,000
CURRENT LIABILITIES	£229,000
NET SALES	£700,000
WORKING CAPITAL	£ 68,000
TOTAL DEBT	£254,000
NET WORTH	£143,000
EARNINGS BEFORE INTEREST AND TAX	£ 24,000
NET PROFIT	£ 15,300
TOTAL ASSETS	£397,000
DEBTORS	£ 85,000
COST OF GOODS SOLD	£500,000
AVERAGE STOCK	£210,000
FIXED ASSETS	£100,000

COMPARISON CHART

BUSINESS NAME: **XYZ Hardware and Building Supply**
BUSINESS ADDRESS: **Anywhere, UK**

DATE PREPARED: **date/month/year**

RATIO TITLE	RATIOS	£ FIGURES	MY RATIOS	INDUSTRY AVERAGES
CURRENT RATIO	CURRENT ASSETS / CURRENT LIABILITIES	£297,000 / £229,000	1.3 times	2.0 times
TURNOVER OF CASH	SALES / WORKING CAPITAL	£700,000 / £68,000	10.3 times	8.1 times
DEBT TO NET WORTH	TOTAL DEBT / NET WORTH	£254,000 / £143,000	1.8 times	1.5 times
NET PROFIT	EARNINGS BEFORE INTEREST & TAX / NET SALES	£24,000 / £700,000	3.4%	Not listed*
RATE OF RETURN ON SALES	NET PROFIT / NET SALES	£15,300 / £700,000	2.2%	3.2%
ROI	NET PROFIT / NET WORTH	£15,300 / £143,000	10.7%	22.7%
ROA	NET PROFIT / TOTAL ASSETS	£15,300 / £397,000	3.8%	8.9%
AVERAGE COLLECTION RATIO	DEBTORS × 365 / SALES	£85,000 × 365 / £700,00	44 days	34.2 days
STOCK TURNOVER	COST OF GOODS SOLD / AVERAGE STOCK	£500,000 / £210,000	2.4 times	5.5 times
FIXED ASSETS TO NET WORTH	FIXED ASSETS / NET WORTH	£100,000 / £143,000	70%	50%
INVESTMENT TURNOVER	NET SALES / TOTAL ASSETS	£700,000 / £397,000	1.8 times	2.9 times

*Not all ratios are listed by all sources. The absence of one or two ratios should not significantly affect your analysis.

DATA GATHERING FORM

BUSINESS NAME: _____

  BUSINESS ADDRESS: _____

DATE PREPARED: _____

ITEMS	£ FIGURES
CURRENT ASSETS	
CURRENT LIABILITIES	
NET SALES	
WORKING CAPITAL	
TOTAL DEBT	
NET WORTH	
EARNINGS BEFORE INTEREST AND TAX	
NET PROFIT	
TOTAL ASSETS	
DEBTORS	
COST OF GOODS SOLD	
AVERAGE STOCK	
FIXED ASSETS	
TOTAL ASSETS	

COMPARISON CHART

BUSINESS NAME: _____

BUSINESS ADDRESS: _____

DATE PREPARED: _____

RATIO TITLE	RATIOS	£ FIGURES	MY RATIOS	INDUSTRY AVERAGES
CURRENT RATIO	$\dfrac{\text{CURRENT ASSETS}}{\text{CURRENT LIABILITIES}}$	_____		
TURNOVER OF CASH	$\dfrac{\text{SALES}}{\text{WORKING CAPITAL}}$	_____		
DEBT TO NET WORTH	$\dfrac{\text{TOTAL DEBT}}{\text{NET WORTH}}$	_____		
NET PROFIT	$\dfrac{\text{EARNINGS BEFORE INTEREST \& TAX}}{\text{NET SALES}}$	_____		
RATE OF RETURN ON SALES	$\dfrac{\text{NET PROFIT}}{\text{NET SALES}}$	_____		
ROI	$\dfrac{\text{NET PROFIT}}{\text{NET WORTH}}$	_____		
ROA	$\dfrac{\text{NET PROFIT}}{\text{TOTAL ASSETS}}$	_____		
AVERAGE COLLECTION RATIO	$\dfrac{\text{DEBTORS} \times 365}{\text{SALES}}$	_____		
STOCK TURNOVER	$\dfrac{\text{COST OF GOODS SOLD}}{\text{AVERAGE STOCK}}$	_____		
FIXED ASSETS TO NET WORTH	$\dfrac{\text{FIXED ASSETS}}{\text{NET WORTH}}$	_____		
INVESTMENT TURNOVER	$\dfrac{\text{NET SALES}}{\text{TOTAL ASSETS}}$	_____		

Ratio review chart

The chart on the next page provides a quick look at how your business is doing. You may discover things that need checking up on because a ratio is too low. The page number for each ratio is listed so that you can refresh your memory as to what each ratio means and how it is derived.

This review chart is intended to help stimulate your thinking and not necessarily to provide answers. To make the best use of it make several copies and complete one each month with those ratios you feel are most important for your business. If your industry averages are normally published quarterly, you may not have them for a month-to-month comparison. However, this chart can provide quick comparisons, and progress can be charted to help keep your business in balance.

Remember, things take time; don't try to achieve too big a correction too quickly as such a move may cause problems in other areas.

RATIO REVIEW CHART

RATIO	YOUR RATIO	INDUSTRY AVERAGE	IF YOUR RATIO IS HIGH	IF YOUR RATIO IS LOW
CURRENT ASSETS / CURRENT LIABILITIES (Pages 34–36)			Check your debt, savings accounts, stock, etc, to see that your money is working for you.	Check stock, debtors and debt structure to see if you can obtain more cash.
SALES / WORKING CAPITAL (Pages 37–39)			Check the ratio above; see if you can obtain more cash.	You may have a cash surplus; invest it in the business, in savings, or pay debts.
TOTAL DEBT / NET WORTH (Pages 40–42)			Check your debt structure, both current and long term.	If too low, you should consider borrowing if the terms are right.
EBIT / NET SALES (Pages 45–47)			Generally, keep up the good work.	See ratio below for effect of interest/ tax.
NET PROFIT / NET SALES (Pages 48–50)			Generally, keep up the good work.	Check expenses and sales expectations.
NET PROFIT / NET WORTH (Pages 51–53)			Check your net worth structure, you could be under-capitalised or a good manager.	Check your debt structure, expenses or operating policies.
NET PROFIT / TOTAL ASSETS (Pages 54–56)			Generally, keep up the good work.	Check your operating policy for asset use.
DEBTORS × 365 / SALES (Pages 58–60)			Check your credit policy.	Generally, keep up the good work.
COST OF GOODS SOLD / AVERAGE STOCK (Pages 61–63)			Could be a good sign; check stock and unfilled sales orders.	Check for over-stocking or obsolete items; check cash flow.
FIXED ASSETS / NET WORTH (Pages 64–66)			Check necessity of fixed assets.	Depends on your type of business.
NET SALES / TOTAL ASSETS (Pages 67–69)			Generally, keep up the good work.	Check necessity for all assets; check whether sales can be increased.

Note: These ratio charts do not take into account the age of a business, the point in the business cycle, local or national economic conditions, or any specific mixes of business. You should consider any one or more of these conditions at the time you are analysing your business.

If one ratio goes up will another always go down?
Sometimes they do, but ratios generally don't work out so neatly.

Sometimes two or more ratios indicate good work and both will be high. Sometimes, depending on your type of business or your point in the business cycle, one will be low, or it won't make any difference what a ratio does.

Ratios are tools to help you analyse a business. In the next two chapters of this book you will be introduced to other techniques that will help you to keep your business in balance. It is important to remember that all tools will never be used all the time. If ratios are used improperly, they could make your position worse.

The proper use of ratios also takes into consideration the economy, the business cycle, and whether your business is just getting started, is achieving growth, or has reached maturity.

Summary

- The first step in determining the interaction between ratios is to transfer the proper figures in pounds for the appropriate items (ie sales, net profit) from your balance sheet and profit and loss account to the data gathering form.

- The second step is to move the figures in pounds from the data gathering form to the comparison chart, then to determine your ratios and place them on the chart.

- The third step is to look up your industry ratio averages and add them to the comparison chart.

- The fourth step is to transfer your ratios and the industry averages to the ratio review chart and compare how your ratios compare with those of your industry. The ratio review chart will provide you with a quick, cursory means of determining what corrective action you should take.

- The fifth step is to plan how to get those of your ratios that are off course back on again . . . and do it!

- All ratios will not be significant to you all the time.

- Ratios will react differently depending on your business' age, where you are in the business cycle, the economic conditions, and your type of business.

CHAPTER 5
How to Perform an Expense Analysis

Expenses are a necessary part of doing business and should be treated as such. Expenses should not be feared or denied. Expenses, however, must be taken into account when developing pricing policies, sales expectations, and a business plan.

Expenses are a fact of life for any business. But expenses that are too high will quickly ruin a business. This may seem obvious, but the point is that expenses must be controlled. The best way to do this is by understanding them; knowing what will result when you increase or decrease an expense.

Examining your expenses

Being familiar with and regularly examining your expenses will help you every day that you are in business. Good expense control can help you to maximise profits on the same or even fewer sales.

A good examination begins with the sales line on your profit and loss account. Understanding why sales did or did not occur as projected will put you in a better position to understand the way in which the expenses of doing business functioned. The first thing to check is whether any particular event took place that month, such as an unusually large sale. Perhaps what should have been a slow month suddenly became a strong one, or vice versa; perhaps bad weather caused shipments to be late and sales suffered. If you were unaware of factors affecting sales, you might overbuy stock after an abnormal non-recurring sale which could result in a fall in profits later on should you have to cut your prices to get rid of old stock.

The sales line

Sales value or income is a function of unit price times unit volume. Therefore, an increase in either will increase sales value. Likewise, if either decreases (with no offsetting increase in the other parameter), sales value will drop. Marking down the price without an offsetting increase in volume will result in lower revenue and almost always a loss of profit. If you planned to get a trade discount to increase your stock for a special sale and money wasn't available in time to claim your discount, then when the merchandise arrived and the customers didn't, you would be in trouble.

The cost of goods sold

The next item to evaluate while examining expenses is the cost of goods sold. Be sensitive to any increase or decrease as a percentage of net sales. Find causes for either an increase or decrease such as: purchased items that increased or decreased in price; increased freight charges; spoilage; or shrinkage due to theft. This area often seems like a 'so what' sort of category, but the success of many businesses can be determined by paying attention to and working out the details on the cost of goods sold line.

The cost of goods sold should be broken down into specific items such as: freight in, manufacturing costs, discounts (taken or not taken) etc. A good review should include going through current invoices and comparing them with past invoices for the same merchandise to determine where the variances are and what caused them.

Credits and collections

There is a cost attached to making money. The trick is to shorten the time between the commitment of cash and the collection of cash. One of the best ways is to review expenses continually.

Fixed expenses (ie expenses whether or not a sale is made)
Let's move on to fixed expenses such as rent, insurance, depreciation, rates and licences. Each fixed expense should be spread in equal monthly installments through the year. If this is done, an increase in sales should cause profit margins to increase at a faster rate than if costs were variable (ie, tied to sales). Fixed expenses can produce a greater return from increased sales than variable expenses. The reverse is also true if sales decrease and expenses are fixed and can't be reduced. Control of expenses, especially fixed expenses, should include the following:

1. Negotiate the best price for all products and services you purchase at the beginning. Practise competitive bidding!
2. Try bartering.
3. Pay only as much and as often as you have to; continually look for better prices.
4. Never pay early unless substantial discounts can be obtained by doing so.
5. Assume that all payment terms are negotiable.
6. Invest — don't spend.

Variable expenses (tied to sales volume)
Variable expenses may include salaries, advertising costs, delivery, supplies, dues and subscriptions, and utilities. These costs should be analysed in relation to their return on sales or other forms of cost efficiency. They are comparable with the 'year to date' figures and percentages. These percentages should be in line with industry percentages and past experience. If sales rise or fall and action is not taken to adjust expenses, closer examination is necessary.

By carefully analysing variable expenses you can determine their value in relation to creating sales or increasing the margin. This is vital when forecasting, or when planning new product lines or expansion, etc.

At the bottom of the statement is net profit.

Net profit may look fine, but there could still be problems because of other variables. If some expense items were reduced and the profit margin did not rise, then something else occurred to offset the logical profit increase. The problem may lie in the cost of goods sold, for example. Remember that it's *pounds collected,* not *pounds'-worth of sales* that you take to the bank. Don't confuse profits with cash flow.

What to do when you can't cut expenses any further

When you run out of cost-cutting ideas, try increasing the return on your expenses. This can be done in several ways including:

1. **Examining your credit policy. Do you:**
   - ☐ Invoice promptly?
   - ☐ Provide clear information about your terms and collection policies?
   - ☐ Maintain an aged debtors schedule and conduct a prompt follow-up on defaulting customers?
   - ☐ Carefully check credit references?

2. **Examining your cash pay-outs. Do you:**
   - ☐ Take advantage of trade discounts?
   - ☐ Pay bills only when they are due?
   - ☐ Try to establish extended and advantageous terms with creditors, such as paying your debt over a long period of time?
   - ☐ Buy only what is needed, when it is needed?

3. **Examining your payroll. Do you:**
   - ☐ Before taking on a new employee consider: overtime? part-time help? temporary help? or freelance workers?
   - ☐ Pay all your employees on the same day?
   - ☐ Consider reducing your salary during slack periods and increasing it during better times?
   - ☐ Check the amount of 'downtime' caused by equipment or other controllable items?
   - ☐ Check starting and finishing times?
   - ☐ Check length of meal and tea breaks
   - ☐ Check petty cash flow?

4. **Examining your stock controls. Do you:**
   - ☐ Check your security to prevent theft?
   - ☐ Instruct your employees about proper handling and storage to prevent breakage and damage to stock?
   - ☐ Calculate in the cost of stock, the cost of storage, handling, insurance, deterioration, obsolescence, etc to make sure you aren't getting a false picture?
   - ☐ Do you regularly check the turnover rate to see whether your stock can be reduced?
   - ☐ Look into just-in-time stock (ie keep your stock levels to a logical minimum)?
   - ☐ Always calculate a level of stock that is relative to your needs?

5. **Examining your manufacturing. Do you:**
   - ☐ Get competitive bids from contractors?
   - ☐ Look into using smaller, less expensive 'cottage suppliers'.
   - ☐ Tighten up planning and scheduling?
   - ☐ Maintain high standards of quality (Redoing work can cost more.)

6. **Examining your marketing plan. Do you:**
   - ☐ Avoid a hit-or-miss approach to advertising and instead target your specific customer group?
   - ☐ Have a clear policy on returns and repairs?
   - ☐ Make sure discounts are going to work, and have a way to end them if they don't?
   - ☐ Train sales people to sell accessory items?
   - ☐ Demand good quality, courteous service for your customers?
   - ☐ Train employees dealing directly with customers to make the most favourable first impression they can?

7. **Examining your purchasing costs. Do you:**
   - ☐ Keep the items purchased to necessities?
   - ☐ Ensure all major purchases are competitively tendered for?
   - ☐ Eliminate unprofitable products from your line?

☐ Look for more efficient ways to 'build' your product?
☐ Maintain good working relationships with your suppliers?

8. **Other areas to examine. Do you:**
   ☐ Use customers' own material?
   ☐ Avoid early payment of expenses, (eg a year's supply of _____ ; or a three-year payment of insurance, etc?)
   ☐ Avoid unnecessary improvements?
   ☐ Avoid unnecessary bulk purchases?
   ☐ Keep good records?
   ☐ Barter?
   ☐ Make cash deposits daily, investing surplus funds in interest-bearing accounts?

Summary

- Expenses are a normal part of doing business and should be considered as such.

- Expenses can and should be controlled so that you know what you are getting for them.

- Begin your expense examination by analysing sales.

- Next look at the cost of goods sold. See if it has increased or decreased, and then find out why.

- Fixed expenses should not vary significantly with any increase or decrease in sales.

- Variable expenses may change with your sales volume.

- When you think you have cut expenses right down to a minimum, there are eight major areas of your business you can examine in order to increase your return on expenses (pages 84–86).

CHAPTER 6
How to Control Your Business

How to proceed

There are several ways to control your business. Some of the best involve financial analysis. This chapter will bring together the use of ratios and percentages and present four basic techniques to help you control your business.

By control, we are talking not only about meeting industry averages, but about helping you to forecast how much money it will take to prepare for a big promotional sale, or introduce a new product line or expand your sales. Control works in two ways. First, it helps you to improve what you are now doing, and second, it helps you to prepare for expansion or change without being caught short of cash because you did not have a plan to keep things in balance.

The four techniques introduced in this chapter are:

1. Trend analysis
2. Cash position charting
3. Target statements
4. Debtors ageing schedule

We will consider each individually.

1. Trend analysis

The data gathering form and the comparison chart which were introduced earlier will aid you in doing a trend analysis. A trend analysis is simply a method of keeping track of month-to-month and year-to-year ratios and expenses. It helps you stay on the right path by alerting you to adjustments you need to make to operate your business successfully.

Four charts found at the end of this section will help you do this. The first keeps track of your ratios from month to month. The second is for tracking your year-to-year ratios. The third is for month-to-month expense tracking. And the fourth is for tracking your year-to-year expenses.

Make a copy of each monthly chart at the beginning of your business year. Label each column with the appropriate name of the month. Record the end-of-month ratios or expenses in the proper column and you will soon have a monthly trend that you can study. Recording end-of-year ratios and expenses on a yearly chart will build up a yearly trend for you. The last column on the chart should list your goal or industry averages for each ratio or expense percentage. This will allow you to chart how well you are progressing.

By keeping track, you have a history of how well you are doing. These records are useful for review and analysis and will help you to plan future action.

The next two charts (pages 89 and 93) are examples of how you can use trends to understand your business better. In our first example, the ratio comparison chart provides a three-year look at the XYZ Hardware and Building Supply Company. Our assumption is that the owner is trying to match the column labelled Industry Average.

XYZ HARDWARE AND BUILDING SUPPLY
RATIO COMPARISON
THREE YEARS

RATIO	1ST YEAR	2ND YEAR	3RD YEAR	INDUSTRY AVERAGE
CURRENT ASSETS / CURRENT LIABILITIES	1.3 ×	1.9 ×	1.9 ×	2.0 ×
SALES / WORKING CAPITAL	10.3 ×	9.7 ×	8.8 ×	8.1 ×
TOTAL DEBT / NET WORTH	1.8 ×	1.5 ×	1.2 ×	1.5 ×
EBIT / NET SALES	3.4%	3.9%	4.0%	Not listed*
NET PROFIT / NET SALES	2.2%	2.4%	2.6%	3.2%
NET PROFIT / NET WORTH	10.7%	14.7%	11.0%	22.7%
NET PROFIT / TOTAL ASSETS	3.8%	4.0%	4.2%	8.9%
DEBTORS × 365 / SALES	44 days	37.7 days	46 days	34.2 days
COST OF GOODS SOLD / AVERAGE STOCK	2.4 ×	3.7 ×	3.4 ×	5.5 ×
FIXED ASSETS / NET WORTH	70%	68.2%	64%	50%
NET SALES / TOTAL ASSETS	1.8 ×	1.6 ×	1.6 ×	2.9 ×

NOTE: × = times; % = per cent; days = average number of days it takes to collect credit sales.

*Not all ratios are listed by all sources. The absence of one or two ratios should not significantly affect your analysis.

COMMENTS

XYZ Hardware and Building Supply ratio comparison analysis

It appears that the current assets to liabilities ratio is moving in the right direction and that the sales to working capital is coming down. Total debt to net worth is below the industry average but still not at the 80 per cent or below recommended figure. The earnings are almost there, and the profit to sales ratio is exceeding the average. The return on investment, however, rose, then fell, and is short of the average.

If the owner wished to get net profit up to the 22.7 per cent average, he or she could increase sales and/or decrease expenses. To continue, the net profit to total assets is also rising, but is still not close to the average. Collection of credit sales was moving in the right direction, then slipped. Perhaps the owner extended the credit terms to increase sales. The turnover did much the same, but dropped, which probably means that the company is still overstocked. The cash position hasn't changed much.

Fixed assets as a part of net worth is staying below the 75 per cent level and dropping to the average of 50 per cent. This may be due in part to the increase in working capital.

The turnover of sales to total assets is not moving towards the averages. This may be due to high stock or more sales may need to be generated for the amount of assets employed. This ratio should also be worked out using fixed assets to see if they are in line.

So there is both good news and bad news for the XYZ Company, but overall, progress is being made. As you review your trends you will want to check back to your original balance sheets and profit and loss accounts, so be sure to save them. The next page summarises the XYZ analysis and suggests actions to improve the business results.

RECOMMENDATIONS

Recommended actions to be taken by the XYZ Hardware and Building Supply Company include:

1. Reducing debt by replacing stock only when absolutely necessary. Apply the savings to pay off loans or the mortgage faster. The money gained from speeding up the collection of debtors can also be used to reduce debt. The reduction of debt should increase net worth because debt should decrease faster than current assets. The reduction of stock and debtors should help the net profit to total asset ratio.
2. Speeding up the collection of debtors will lower the average days collection period. If credit terms were previously extended to increase sales, it doesn't appear to have helped. If this was done, credit terms need to be changed (ie, tightened).
3. Slowing down stock purchasing. The stock turnover ratio should improve.
4. Shrinking total assets should improve the sales to total assets ratio. However, increasing sales is a better way to do it.

Now let's see how expenses look.

COMMENTS

XYZ Hardware and Building Supply expense analysis

The cost of goods sold ratio is holding steady and is close to the industry average, even as sales climb. Sales have increased each year by over 3 per cent, but gross profit did not keep pace. This could be attributed to the owner not taking advantage of volume discounts or trade discounts or perhaps this is the nature of the business. The salary of the owner is roughly triple the industry average, which is part of the reason why there is a lack of working capital. This may also be a contributing factor as to why creditors are larger than they should be.

Employee salaries are coming in line with the industry average. This should be kept an eye on to ensure that the trend does not reverse itself.

Delivery expenses are close to average, as is the bad debt figure. The drop in bad debt in the third year may indicate better credit control and should be encouraged. Telephone and depreciation expenses are on target. Insurance payments seem high compared to the industry average and should be checked to see if the amount of coverage is really necessary. Meeting the industry average would add over £1,000 to profit. Advertising is low but sales are rising. Sales may go up faster with more publicity. Net profit is falling in spite of rising sales, but is better than the industry average which shows a loss.

RECOMMENDATIONS
1. Check gross profit by investigating volume and/or trade discounts.
2. Keep up the good work on holding expenses down.
3. Look into insurance payments to see whether these could be lowered.
4. And keep a eye on employee expenses as sales rise.

XYZ HARDWARE AND BUILDING SUPPLY
EXPENSE SHEET
THREE YEAR COMPARISON

EXPENSE ITEM	1ST YEAR		2ND YEAR		3RD YEAR		INDUSTRY AVERAGE
	AMOUNT IN £s	%	AMOUNT IN £s	%	AMOUNT IN £s	%	%
SALES	700,000	100	725,000	100	750,000	100	100
COST OF GOODS SOLD	500,000	71	522,000	72	540,000	72	72.46
GROSS PROFIT	200,000	29	203,000	28	210,000	28	27.54
% INCREASE IN SALES		3.4		3.3			
SALARY (OWNER)	74,000	10.6	74,000	10.2	74,000	9.9	3.84
WAGES	65,000	9.3	65,000	9.0	75,000	10.0	10.43
DELIVERY	7,000	1.0	11,000	1.5	9,000	1.2	1.40
BAD DEBT	4,000	.6	4,000	.6	4,000	.5	.77
TELEPHONE	2,000	.3	2,000	.3	2,600	.3	.35
DEPRECIATION	4,000	.6	4,000	.6	4,000	.5	.58
INSURANCE	7,000	1.0	7,300	1.0	7,500	1.0	.80
RATES	8,000	1.1	8,000	1.1	8,000	1.1	.27
INTEREST	8,700	1.2	8,700	1.2	8,700	1.2	1.71
ADVERTISING	3,000	.4	4,000	.5	5,200	.7	.94
MISCELLANEOUS	2,000	.3	2,500	.3	4,000	.5	6.96*
	£184,700	26.4	£190,500	26.3	£202,000	26.9	28.05
NET PROFIT	15,300	2.2	12,900	1.7	8,000	1.1	(.51)

*Miscellaneous includes donations, office and shop supplies, rent and rates, credit card expenses, leasing, legal and accounting, computer services, dues and subscriptions, entertainment, laundry, waste disposal, employee benefits, and other.

COMMENTS

A yearly example was used for this analysis, but it could have been monthly. In your analysis you should complete both, since most businesses rise and fall substantially during a year's business cycle and comparing similar months year-by-year can be useful.

End-of-year figures are most commonly used to make trend charts. However, if one particular month in your business cycle provides a more significant period of time, use that month as your starting point for yearly figures. Remember to start with the same month each time you prepare your yearly chart so that your comparisons are meaningful.

These numbers *must be coupled with experience and common sense to be of value*. A ratio consists of two figures. To change it you can raise one, lower the other, or do both. There is usually more than one choice. Before taking action, check (using target numbers) to see what effect your action may have on other ratios as some figures are used in more than one ratio. Following this page, there are the four blank forms (pages 95–98), which you can copy and use to analyse your trends.

Note: The forms on pages 95–98 may be copied by permission of the publisher for personal use only.

RATIO COMPARISON BY MONTH

BUSINESS NAME _____

BUSINESS ADDRESS _____

RATIO	MONTH					
$\dfrac{\text{CURRENT ASSETS}}{\text{CURRENT LIABILITIES}}$						
$\dfrac{\text{SALES}}{\text{WORKING CAPITAL}}$						
$\dfrac{\text{TOTAL DEBT}}{\text{NET WORTH}}$						
$\dfrac{\text{EBIT}}{\text{SALES}}$						
$\dfrac{\text{NET PROFIT}}{\text{NET SALES}}$						
$\dfrac{\text{NET PROFIT}}{\text{NET WORTH}}$						
$\dfrac{\text{NET PROFIT}}{\text{TOTAL ASSETS}}$						
$\dfrac{\text{DEBTORS} \times 365}{\text{SALES}}$						
$\dfrac{\text{COST OF GOODS SOLD}}{\text{AVERAGE STOCK}}$						
$\dfrac{\text{FIXED ASSETS}}{\text{NET WORTH}}$						
$\dfrac{\text{NET SALES}}{\text{TOTAL ASSETS}}$						

RATIO COMPARISON BY YEAR

BUSINESS NAME _____

BUSINESS ADDRESS _____

RATIO	YEAR					
CURRENT ASSETS / CURRENT LIABILITIES						
SALES / WORKING CAPITAL						
TOTAL DEBT / NET WORTH						
EBIT / SALES						
NET PROFIT / NET SALES						
NET PROFIT / NET WORTH						
NET PROFIT / TOTAL ASSETS						
DEBTORS × 365 / SALES						
COST OF GOODS SOLD / AVERAGE STOCK						
FIXED ASSETS / NET WORTH						
NET SALES / TOTAL ASSETS						

EXPENSE COMPARISON BY MONTH

MY BUSINESS: _____

BUSINESS ADDRESS: _____

MONTH							
EXPENSE ITEM	AMOUNT IN £s	%	AMOUNT IN £s	%	AMOUNT IN £s	%	INDUSTRY AVERAGE
SALES							
COST OF GOODS SOLD							
GROSS PROFIT							
% INC (DEC) IN SALES							
SALARY (OWNER)							
WAGES							
DELIVERY							
BAD DEBT							
TELEPHONE							
DEPRECIATION							
INSURANCE							
RATES							
INTEREST							
ADVERTISING							
MISCELLANEOUS							
NET PROFIT BEFORE TAX							

EXPENSE COMPARISON BY YEAR

MY BUSINESS: _____

BUSINESS ADDRESS: _____

MONTH							
EXPENSE ITEM	AMOUNT IN £s	%	AMOUNT IN £s	%	AMOUNT IN £s	%	INDUSTRY AVERAGE
SALES							
COST OF GOODS SOLD							
GROSS PROFIT							
% INC (DEC) IN SALES							
SALARY (OWNER)							
WAGES							
DELIVERY							
BAD DEBT							
TELEPHONE							
DEPRECIATION							
INSURANCE							
RATES							
INTEREST							
ADVERTISING							
MISCELLANEOUS							
NET PROFIT BEFORE TAX							

2. Cash position charting

If there is only one thing you remember from this book, make it this: *Never run out of cash!*

In a small business a lack of cash, even for a short time, can cause all your work and planning to become worthless. A cash shortage is the one thing that is most difficult to overcome. If you can't pay your bills, your staff or yourself, you won't be in business very long *even if you are showing a profit on paper*.

To help avoid this situation, especially when planning to do something different (such as expanding your business or taking on a new product line), a cash position chart will be of immeasurable value. This chart will help you to target when cash will be needed to pay bills. It will also help you to determine where to obtain cash to support items such as expansion, (for example, speeding up debtors collection, increasing cash sales, or borrowing). The cash position chart deals *only* with cash — cash paid out and cash taken in. It helps to identify those periods when borrowing must be considered. This allows you to make arrangements for the cash *before* you actually need it. Pre-planning works wonders when talking to bankers.

An estimated cash position chart should be made a year in advance. A second chart should be used to record total cash income and expenditure on a weekly or monthly basis. By keeping track of the outflow and inflow of cash and comparing these actual figures to your estimates, your budgeting ability will greatly improve. You will have good documents to show whether you need to seek new money. Another version would be to make two columns for each month, one would be for the estimate, the other for the actual. This method has the advantage of checking the accuracy of your estimates on one chart. Both types of chart are shown at the end of this section. The cash position chart on page 101 shows estimates for the opening month plus the next five months.

In making your cash position chart, follow the example on page 101. In the first column list the starting cash that you believe will be available at the *end* of the opening month. In the example shown, it is £200. Next, list the cash sales at the end of the month (£3,550 in our example). Then list the cash received from previous sales (£550 in our example) in the opening month. This provides a total inflow of cash of £4,100.

To determine cash outflow, list what you believe your expenses will be. In the example the expenses are: £1,000 purchases, £600 rent, £2,050 wages, and £350 for miscellaneous expenses, for a total cash outflow of £4,000. Next add total cash inflow to the starting cash balance and then subtract the total cash outflow to obtain the closing balance, which is £300 in the example.

The cash position is found by subtracting the total cash outflow from the total cash inflow, which makes £100 in our example. Here we are interested only in the amount of cash created or lost during the opening month. A loss is shown by the pound figure in brackets ( ); a loss of £25 would be shown as (25).

Take the closing balance and place it at the top of the chart as the first month's starting cash figure. In our example this is £300. Then record the end-of-the-month totals for cash inflow and cash outflow. The closing balance comes from adding the starting cash, £300, to the cash inflow £3,450, for a balance of £3,750, and subtracting total cash outflow from it (£3,950) for a closing balance in the first month of a negative £200, shown as (200). The cash flow for the first month is cash outflow subtracted from cash inflow, or a negative £500, shown as (500).

The first month's closing balance becomes the second month's starting cash (a negative £200). After the second month's closing totals are written in, our example shows that the closing balance is a positive £100. In other words, the cash position has changed to a positive £300 and stays positive, as the cash sales and credit collections increase and expenses remain stable.

In the second month the projected closing balance and cash position both become positive.

CASH POSITION CHART

MONTHS

ITEMS	OPENING	1ST	2ND	3RD	4TH	5TH
STARTING CASH	200	300	(200)	100	400	600
CASH INFLOW						
CASH SALES	3,550	2,950	4,000	3,300	3,000	3,200
CASH RECEIVED	550	500	1,550	1,800	2,000	2,000
TOTAL CASH INFLOW	4,100	3,450	5,550	5,100	5,000	5,200
CASH OUTFLOW						
PURCHASES	1,000	1,000	2,500	2,000	2,000	2,000
RENT	600	600	600	600	600	600
WAGES	2,050	2,050	2,050	2,050	2,050	2,050
MISCELLANEOUS	350	300	100	150	150	150
TOTAL CASH OUTFLOW	4,000	3,950	5,250	4,800	4,800	4,800
NET CASH FLOW	300	(200)	100	400	600	1,000
CASH POSITION	100	(500)	300	300	200	400

Note: ( ) means a loss or negative cash position. Your chart will be much more detailed than this example, which was shortened to simplify the explanation.

The cash position chart can also be used for planning cash positions; the following two examples (pages 102 and 103) provide a brief demonstration. For instance, you might want to consider borrowing instead of running a negative closing balance in the second month. The example on page 103 shows what would happen if you borrowed £200 in the opening month.

Planning cash positions

Let's look at the example on the following page. By starting with cash of £400, and keeping everything else the same, we see that there is no negative net cash flow. But note the cash position is the same as in the example above. This is because the difference between our cash inflow and cash outflow did not change. We start recording a positive cash position at the end of the second month as before.

CASH POSITION CHART

MONTHS

ITEMS	OPENING	1ST	2ND	3RD	4TH	5TH
STARTING CASH	400*	500	0	300	600	800
CASH INFLOW						
CASH SALES	3,550	2,950	4,000	3,300	3,000	3,200
CASH RECEIVED	550	500	1,550	1,800	2,000	2,000
TOTAL CASH INFLOW	4,100	3,450	5,550	5,100	5,000	5,200
CASH OUTFLOW						
PURCHASES	1,000	1,000	2,500	2,000	2,000	2,000
RENT	600	600	600	600	600	600
WAGES	2,050	2,050	2,050	2,050	2,050	2,050
MISCELLANEOUS	350	300	100	150	150	150
TOTAL CASH OUTFLOW	4,000	3,950	5,250	4,800	4,800	4,800
NET CASH FLOW	500	0	300	600	800	1,200
CHANGE IN CASH POSITION	100	(500)	300	300	200	400

Notes: *Assumes £200 has been borrowed.
( ) means a loss or negative cash position.
Your chart will be much more detailed than this example which was shortened to simplify the explanation.
Interest paid on the loan would be an expense each month until paid. In this example it was not shown.

If you didn't want to borrow but wanted a positive closing balance and cash position, you could collect your debtors faster, reduce expenses, or postpone other expenses such as employing new staff. To see what happens if we reduce purchasing by £500 in the first month and second month, study the example opposite. The closing balance stays positive. Cash flow breaks even in the first month and also stays positive. If purchases could be reduced (perhaps increased at a later date) there would not be a negative cash position and this action could keep your cash flow positive and your business healthy.

CASH POSITION CHART

MONTHS

ITEMS	OPENING	1ST	2ND	3RD	4TH	5TH
STARTING CASH	200	300	300	1,100	1,400	1,600
CASH INFLOW						
CASH SALES	3,550	2,950	4,000	3,300	3,000	3,200
CASH RECEIVED	550	500	1,550	1,800	2,000	2,000
TOTAL CASH INFLOW	4,100	3,450	5,550	5,100	5,000	5,200
CASH OUTFLOW						
PURCHASES	1,000	500	2,000	2,000	2,000	2,000
RENT	600	600	600	600	600	600
WAGES	2,050	2,050	2,050	2,050	2,050	2,050
MISCELLANEOUS	350	300	100	150	150	150
TOTAL CASH OUTFLOW	4,000	3,450	4,750	4,800	4,800	4,800
NET CASH FLOW	300	300	1,100	1,400	1,600	2,000
CASH POSITION	100	0	800	300	200	400

> *Note:* ( ) means a loss or negative cash position.
> Your chart will be much more detailed than this example,
> which was shortened to simplify the explanation.

By using a cash position chart you can keep your business solvent and learn your lessons on paper (not the hard way).

Pages 104 and 105 show cash position charts. Improve your cash position by using one of them. These may be copied by permission of the publisher.

CASH POSITION CHART

BUSINESS NAME _____

BUSINESS ADDRESS _____

	MONTH	MONTH	MONTH	MONTH	MONTH	MONTH
BEGINNING OF MONTH Cash on hand						
Cash in bank						
Other cash						
TOTAL CASH						
INCOME DURING MONTH Cash sales						
Credit sales receipts						
Investment income						
Other income						
TOTAL INCOME						
EXPENSES DURING MONTH Purchases (Stock)						
Owners salary						
Salaries						
Other payroll costs — N.1. etc						
Repairs/maintenance						
Selling expense						
Transport						
Loan payment						
Office supplies						
Utilities						
Telephone						
Dues/subscriptions						
Depreciation						
Advertising						
Rent						
Rates						
Insurance						
Legal/accounting						
Other						
TOTAL EXPENSES **END OF MONTH**						
END OF MONTH **BALANCE (LOSS)**						
CHANGE IN CASH **POSITION MONTHLY**						

CASH POSITION CHART

BUSINESS NAME _____

BUSINESS ADDRESS _____

	MONTH		MONTH		MONTH	
	BUDGET	ACTUAL	BUDGET	ACTUAL	BUDGET	ACTUAL
BEGINNING OF MONTH Cash on hand						
Cash in bank						
Other cash						
TOTAL CASH						
INCOME DURING MONTH Cash sales						
Credit sales receipts						
Investment income						
Other income						
TOTAL INCOME						
EXPENSES DURING MONTH Purchases (Stock)						
Owners salary						
Salaries						
Other payroll costs — N.1. etc						
Repairs/maintenance						
Selling expense						
Transport						
Loan payment						
Office supplies						
Utilities						
Telephone						
Dues/subscriptions						
Depreciation						
Advertising						
Rent						
Rates						
Insurance						
Legal/accounting						
Other						
TOTAL EXPENSES END OF MONTH						
END OF MONTH **BALANCE (LOSS)**						
CHANGE IN CASH POSITION MONTHLY						

3. Development of a target statement

A target statement is sometimes called a pro-forma statement. It is a model (or ideal) of the balance sheet and profit and loss account. It is an ideal because it is one that you wish to achieve. To create a target statement, begin by comparing your balance sheet and profit and loss account percentages with those of your industry *or* those you wish to achieve.

On pages 108 and 109 is a sample of a balance sheet and profit and loss account of the XYZ Hardware and Building Supply Company which includes the percentages of all figures. Also listed is the target statement. In the example shown, the percentages of the industry are marked as industry averages (IA). The balance sheet percentages are percentages of the totals of the assets and liabilities columns respectively, shown as CA & FA (total current assets and fixed assets) and LIABILITIES & NW (total liabilities and net worth). The profit and loss account shows the percentage of net sales. Let's assume that the owner wants to compare his or her averages with those of the industry.

Of course, any target could be used instead of the industry averages. From the example, note that the cash and stock percentages are way off course. The owner needs to reduce stock to gain more cash. Note that the total current asset percentages are very close. The difference is in the mix of current assets.

On the liability side, the owner's bills, shown as creditors, haven't been paid on time as indicated by the big difference between the statement percentages and the industry average percentages. This is probably due to a lack of cash flow or positive cash position.

The profit and loss account also needs adjustment. The cost of goods sold is a little off course. Perhaps this is because of the owner's inability to take advantage of trade or bulk discounts, or possibly he or she is purchasing goods from a high cost supplier. The expenses could also do with being brought into line. For instance, the advertising expense is very low. If increased, it might help to promote greater sales, which in turn would lower the stock and eventually gain some much needed cash. Also, the owner's salary is too high for the current circumstances.

Once targets have been selected, trying different combinations of sales, expenses, etc should enable you to see what you need to do to achieve the financial position that is your goal.

Remember that reality-based experience must be used in making target statements. For instance, you probably won't jump 50 per cent in sales or reduce expenses by half overnight. Don't expect instant results when experience tells you this won't happen. Steady progress towards your goal is the answer. Balance your approach. You can't sacrifice one element for very long without causing more problems somewhere else.

Develop your own target statement by using your balance sheets and profit and loss accounts. Place a column on both reports, one for your averages and another column for your targets. Then compare the two. Determine the figures you need to meet your targets for each line item.

The use of ratios and a cash position chart will help you to develop your strategy. Your approach should take into consideration the age of your business, the condition of the economy, your competition, and the nature of your business. Things take time, but if you keep your business finances in balance, you will not only survive, you should prosper.

XYZ HARDWARE AND BUILDING SUPPLY
BALANCE SHEET
YEAR END 19XX

ASSETS

	£		%	IA%
CASH	2,000		0.5	7.7
DEBTORS	85,000		21.4	27.5
STOCK	210,000		52.9	37.2
TOTAL CA		297,000	74.8	74.4
LAND/BLDG	50,000			
EQUIP/FIX	50,000			
TOTAL FA		100,000	25.2	25.6
CA AND FA		397,000	100.0	100.0

LIABILITIES

	£		%	IA%
NOTES PAYABLE	18,000		4.5	9.7
CREDITORS	205,000		51.7	17.7
ACCRUALS	6,000		1.5	–
TOTAL CL		229,000	57.7	39.1
MORTGAGE	25,000			
TOTAL LTD		25,000	6.3	17.8
NET WORTH		143,000	36.0	40.7
LIABILITIES AND NW		397,000	100.0	100.0

CA = current assets; BLDG = buildings; EQUIP = equipment; FIX = fixtures; CA = current assets; FA = fixed assets; NW = net worth; CL = current liabilities; LTD = long-term debt.
*IA% = industry averages.

Explanation of the contents included in the industry averages

Included in total CA are 2 per cent of all other current assets.

Included in total FA are 0.3 per cent intangibles and 4.5 per cent of all other non-current.

Included in total CL are current maturing LTD 3.4 per cent; income tax payable 0.8 per cent; and all other current 7.6 per cent.

Included in LIAB and NW are deferred tax 0.5 per cent and other non-current 1.9 per cent.

XYZ HARDWARE AND BUILDING SUPPLY
PROFIT AND LOSS ACCOUNT
FOR THE YEAR OF 19____

					%	IA%
NET SALES (LESS ALLOW & DISCOUNTS)				£700,000	100.0	100.00
COST OF GOODS SOLD				500,000	71.4	72.46
GROSS PROFIT				200,000	28.6	27.54
EXPENSES		%	IA%			
SALARY (OWNER)	£ 74,000	10.6	3.84			
WAGES	65,000	9.3	10.43			
DELIVERY	7,000	1.0	1.40			
BAD DEBT	4,000	.6	1.77			
TELEPHONE	2,000	.3	.35			
DEPRECIATION	4,000	.6	.58			
INSURANCE	7,000	1.0	.80			
RATES	8,000	1.1	.27			
INTEREST	8,700	1.2	1.71			
ADVERTISING	3,000	.4	.94			
MISCELLANEOUS	2,000	.3	6.96*			
TOTAL EXPENSES	184,000	26.4	28.5			
					%	IA%
NET PROFIT (BEFORE TAX)				£15,300	2.2	(.51)

* Miscellaneous includes donations, office and shop supplies, credit card expenses, leasing, legal and accounting, computer services, dues and subscriptions, entertainment, laundry, waste disposal, employee benefits, and other.

4. Debtors ageing schedule

The debtors ageing schedule is a control technique that can save you both money and headaches. It is a simple tool. Just keep a record, as shown on page 111, as a reminder of customers who still owe you money. A timely follow-up, with an appropriate overdue notice to defaulting customers, can retrieve an account that may otherwise have been 'forgotten' forever.

The table below provides an indication that the longer you wait to collect your debtors, the less likely you are to receive full payment.

This table of collection likelihood for debtors assumes that you have the correct information concerning the address for a customer or the address and credit check for a business buying finished goods or raw materials.

Past date due by:	Probability of collection
30 days	95 per cent
60 days	82 per cent
120 days	70 per cent
6 months	49.5 per cent

DEBTORS AGEING SCHEDULE
XYZ HARDWARE AND BUILDING SUPPLY

DEBTORS AGEING SCHEDULE					
			PAST DATE DUE BY		
CUSTOMER	TOTAL	CURRENT	30–59 DAYS	60–119 DAYS	120–180 DAYS
A	5,000	3,000	2,000		
B	2,000	1,000		1,000	
C	1,000	1,000			
D	4,000	1,000		3,000	
E	3,000	1,000	500	500	1,000
F	12,000	10,000	2,000		
G	3,000	2,000		1,000	
H	5,000	3,000	1,000	1,000	
I	3,000	3,000			
J	2,000	2,000			
K	10,000	10,000			
L	3,000	2,000			1,000
M	7,000	5,000		2,000	
N	2,000	2,000			
O	8,000	7,000	1,000		
P	6,000	3,000	3,000		
Q	6,000		500	4,500	1,000
R	3,000			1,000	2,000
TOTAL	85,000	56,000	10,000	14,000	5,000
PER CENT	100%	66%	12%	16%	6%

Note: Days refers to calendar days not working days.

Summary

Tick those that you intend to use:

☐ A trend analysis is an excellent technique to help me measure the direction in which my business is going.

☐ A month-by-month and year-by-year comparison will accurately develop the trend my business is taking.

☐ I plan never to run out of cash.

☐ Cash position charting will help me to forecast when and how much money I will need to carry out my plans.

☐ A target statement is the development of a balance sheet and a profit and loss account as a 'target' which I wish to achieve.

☐ The debtors ageing schedule is a must if I do business on credit.

☐ The debtors ageing schedule will help to remind me of accounts that are past their due date and require special attention.

Further Reading
from Kogan Page

Better Management Skills

Creative Thinking in Business, Carol Kinsey Goman

Delegating for Results, Robert B Maddux

Effective Employee Participation, Lynn Tylczak

Effective Meeting Skills: How to Make Meetings More Productive, Marion E Haynes

Effective Performance Appraisals, Robert B Maddux

Effective Presentation Skills, Steve Mandel

The Fifty-Minute Supervisor: A Guide for the Newly Promoted, Elwood N Chapman

How to Communicate Effectively, Bert Decker

How to Develop Assertiveness, Sam R Lloyd

How to Motivate People, Twyla Dell

Improving Relations at Work, Elwood N Chapman

Leadership Skills for Women, Marilyn Manning and Patricia Haddock

Make Every Minute Count: How to Manage Your Time Effectively, Marion E Haynes

Managing Disagreement Constructively, Herbert S Kindler

Managing Organisational Change, Cynthia D Scott and Dennis T Jaffe

Managing Quality Customer Service, William B Martin

Project Management, Marion E Haynes

Risk Taking, Herbert S Kindler

Successful Negotiation, Robert B Maddux

Systematic Problem-Solving and Decision-Making, Sandy Pokras

Team Building: An Exercise in Leadership, Robert B Maddux

Other titles
Accounting for Non-Accountants, Graham Mott
Baffled by Balance Sheets? William Lee Johnson
The Cash Collection Action Kit, Philip Gegan and Jane Harrison
How to Understand the Financial Press, John Andrew

69   25